NOR WAY

Travel with Marco Polo Insider Tips

INSIDER TIP
Your shortcut to a great experience

MARCO POLO
TOP HIGHLIGHTS

HOLMENKOLLEN 1
The ski jump (photo) on the outskirts of Oslo has acquired cult status. From the top, there are extensive views of the surrounding area.

➤ p. 44, The South

PREIKESTOLEN 2
The rocky plateau at Lysefjord must be the most beautiful viewing point in western Norway.
📷 *Tip: If you get up early, you'll be rewarded with an undisturbed view (it gets particularly busy around midday).*

➤ p. 63, The West

BRYGGEN 3
The warehouse quarter at the harbour in Bergen is more than just a testament to the city's Hanseatic heyday.
📷 *Tip: You can best capture the charm of the Middle Ages if you take photos without the flash.*

➤ p. 66, The West

THE FLÅM RAILWAY 4
An exciting train journey through high mountains to the fjord.
📷 *Tip: Sit on the right-hand side when travelling towards Flåm and get your camera ready for when the train goes round a bend.*

➤ p. 72, The West

GEIRANGERFJORD 5
Discover Norway's storybook fjord from the water or from a great height.
📷 *Tip: If you hike to the 320m-high Westerås farm, you will discover a breathtaking panorama before your lens.*

➤ p. 75, The West

NIDAROS CATHEDRAL 6
Norway's national sanctuary in Trondheim is the largest medieval building in Scandinavia.

➤ p. 84, Trøndelag

SALTSTRAUMEN ⭐

The view from the bridge may make you dizzy: the water speeds through the strait near Bodø four times per day.

➤ p. 96, The North

ANDENES ⭐ 8

The Vesterålen island of Andøya is surrounded by snow-white beaches.

📷 *Tip: It's worth having a good lens if you go on a whale-watching safari, but protect your camera from the saltwater!*

➤ p. 108, Lofoten & Vesterålen

ALTA MUSEUM ⭐ 9

Kilometres of walks along the ancient rock carvings, made from 2,000 to 7,000 years ago.

➤ p. 122, Finnmark

THE NORTH CAPE ⭐ 10

Spending a summer night under clear skies where the sun barely touches the sea is an unforgettable experience.

➤ p. 124, Finnmark

CONTENTS

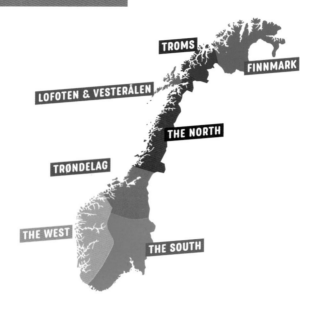

TROMS
FINNMARK
LOFOTEN & VESTERÅLEN
THE NORTH
TRØNDELAG
THE WEST
THE SOUTH

🕙 Plan your visit

£-£££ Price categories

(*) Premium rate phone number

🍴 Eating/drinking

👜 Shopping

🍸 Going out

(🕮 A2) Refers to the removable pull-out map
(🕮 a2) Refers to the inset street maps on the pull-out map
(0) Located off the map

BEST OF
NORWAY

Fairytale scenery at Geirangerfjord

BEST

WHEN IT RAINS

ACTIVITIES TO BRIGHTEN YOUR DAY

TREASURE IN THE SILVER MOUNTAIN

Visit the *Norwegian Mining Museum* (photo) and travel an exciting 2.3km into the heart of the mountain on the pit railway that runs through Kongsberg's old silver mine. You won't care what the weather's doing above ground for a while.

➤ p.48, The South

UNDER GLASS

Going to Hamar when it's raining is a great idea. The *ruins of the cathedral* are protected by an impressive glass pyramid. If you go inside, you'll experience the special atmosphere of the place undisturbed by the weather.

➤ p.51, The South

PENGUINS & CROCODILES

In Bergen, it's always worth having a plan B. However, the *Akvariet* is more than just a back-up solution for when it's raining: not only will you come across penguins and seals in the aquarium, but also snakes and crocodiles.

➤ p.67, The West

HUNT, SHOP, LOOK

You can outwit the bad weather in *Devoldfabrikken* in Ålesund. As well as the famous Devold pullovers, the factory shop sells many other items, so take the time to browse. And then there is the café with a wonderful view of the islands offshore…

➤ p.75, The West

RAINY DAY REFRESHMENT

Sweet things bring joy, even north of the Arctic Circle. In the *Melkebaren* café in Bodø, you can enjoy your ice cream while the rain pours down in sheets outside. If you prefer something warm, they also serve a wide range of speciality coffees.

➤ p. 93, The North

BEST 🐷
ON A BUDGET

FOR SMALLER WALLETS

MONUMENTAL ART IN THE PARK
Art appreciation with a picnic: take your time to admire the famous sculptures in the *Vigelandsparken* (photo), which is part of Frognerparken, one of the most popular places in the capital for meeting up with friends in the summer.
➤ p.44, The South

BIRD'S EYE VIEW
What is perhaps the most spectacular view in mainland Norway will cost you nothing. Just walk out to the edge of the *Stegasteinen* lookout, a viewing platform that resembles a ski jump at a dizzying height of 650m. If you're not afraid of heights, you'll definitely enjoy this view of the Aurlandsfjord.
➤ p.72, The West

TWIST YOUR WAY UP THE COAST
The *Atlantic Ocean Route* is the most unusual road to explore in Norway. It snakes its way along the coast over bridges and across islands; you can even fish from lay-bys, and the gusting wind will make you think you're at sea. The entire route is toll-free.
➤ p.77, The West

THINKING OUTSIDE THE BOX
The *Perspektivet Museum* provides impressive photo documentation for those interested in the landscape, culture and history of Northern Norway. Dive in and immerse yourself in the different eras.
➤ p.115, Troms

NO SORCERY HERE
Although it cost £8.5 million to build, the *Steilneset Minnested* (Witches' Memorial) in Vardø is free to visit. Designed by the Swiss architect Peter Zumthor, the monument stands as a reminder of Norway's witch-hunting past.
➤ p.125, Finnmark

BEST WITH CHILDREN

FUN FOR YOUNG & OLD

JUST DIVE IN
When the weather is kind, the many water attractions at *Bø Sommarland* (photo) in Telemark are wonderful and will soon tire everyone out!
➤ p.55, The South

LOOKING FOR TREASURE
Whether you're digging for gold, looking for treasure with a secret map or finding gemstones, an afternoon at the *Mineral Park* will go by in a flash. There are guided worshops where the whole family can use a variety of tools to make stone figures – great souvenirs to take home.
➤ p.57, The South

FOR KNOWLEDGE SEEKERS
How does an oil platform work? What does the Gulf Stream on the coast have to do with rain clouds on the mountain slopes? The *VilVite* science centre in Bergen provides answers to questions about the weather, environment and energy.
➤ p.69, The West

FASCINATION FOR THE SEA
At the *Atlantic Sea Park* science centre in Ålesund, young researchers can set about deciphering the secrets of the sea – but not all of them; they'll also learn that 95% of sea life is still a mystery.
➤ p.75, The West

YOUNG POLAR RESEARCHERS
How do you prepare for a polar expedition? Documentaries at *Polaria's* wide-screen cinema provide some initial answers. There's also an aquarium and seals.
➤ p. 115, Troms

BEST ⚑
CLASSIC EXPERIENCES

SKIING ON HIGH
You don't have to be interested in ski jumping to enjoy a visit to the *Holmenkollen* ski jump. First visit the Ski Museum; afterwards, the magnificent view will take your breath away.
➤ p.44, The South

EPIC PERFORMANCE
Peer Gynt, the hero in Henrik Ibsen's dramatic play, is the embodiment of how Norwegians see themselves: adventurous but narrow-minded, imaginative but brutally down to earth. For a classic performance, head to the *Peer Gynt Festival* which is held in the beautiful countryside around Gålåvatnet Lake.
➤ p.53, The South

CARVED OUT IN THE ICE AGE
Discover the sky and the water in a whole new light. Norway's fjords are the link between the coast and the *fjell*. One particularly beautiful inlet awaits you at the Lysefjord near Stavanger, with a breathtaking view from *Preikestolen* (Pulpit Rock) (photo).
➤ p.63, The West

CHURCHES WITH PAGAN CHARM
The stave churches, with their pagan decoration, are a magnificent reminder of early Christianity. On no account should you miss the famous *Borgund Stavkirke* near Lærdal on the Sognefjord.
➤ p.71, The West

NATIONAL PRIDE
Fresh birch twigs are an essential part of *Constitution Day*, a Norwegian national holiday on 17 May. Try to be in Oslo on that day: the celebrations in the capital are especially charming, with a children's procession past the palace.
➤ p.139, Festivals & events

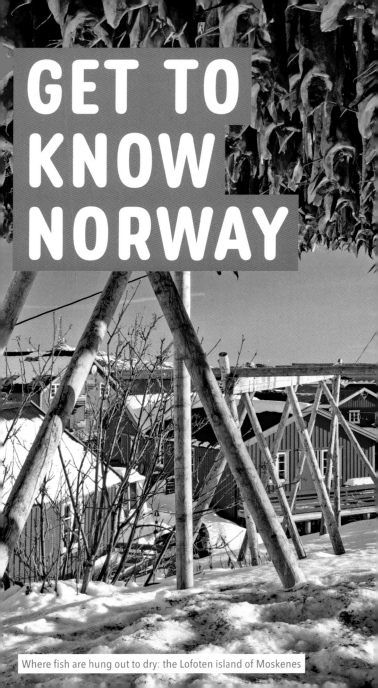

GET TO KNOW NORWAY

Where fish are hung out to dry: the Lofoten island of Moskenes

DISCOVER NORWAY

A nice place for a stroll on a summer's evening: Aker Brygge on Oslofjord

Once a year the world turns its attention to the northern corner of Europe, when the winner of the Nobel Peace Prize is announced. When choosing the recipient, the Nobel Committee, appointed by the Norwegian parliament, seeks to shed light on a particular crisis, which can be controversial.

AMIABLE ACHIEVERS

But Norway does not have to go looking for friends; it can make it on its own. The country is ranked number one on many lists: it's the country with the least corruption, the best quality of life, and the most advanced climate policies. These best-in-class Norwegians are showing the rest of the world how it's done. But that's not all – they also have a popular royal family.

793–1066 CE
Viking Era

c. 1250
The Hanseatic League establishes outposts and exploits the country

1397–1905
Kalmar Union between Denmark, Sweden and Norway; from 1814, Union with Sweden

1905
Norway's independence, foundation of the Constitution in Eidsvoll (17 May)

1940–45
The German Wehrmacht occupies Norway

Mid-1960s
First promising oil discovery in the North Sea

OIL WEALTH

The oil boom enabled Norway to invest enormous sums of money in its deeply rooted social democracy and egalitarian policies. These are a reflection of the Nordic value of *Janteloven* – or the *Law of Jante* – a sociological term used to describe a belief that nobody is better than anybody else. The money generated from oil and gas (Norway is still the world's fifth-largest exporter of oil and Europe's second-largest exporter of gas) is invested into a sovereign wealth fund, and the country has virtually no debt whatsoever.

One of the major challenges this century has been to connect up this vast country. Norway's broadband connectivity has been a resounding success; there is mobile connection in even the most isolated *fjell*. However, the transport infrastructure project is taking a bit longer: roads and railways are still under construction between Fredrikstad and Kirkenes; bridges are being built over the fjord to partly replace the ferries; while tunnels are continually being drilled into the Norway's endless mountain ranges. When it comes to building tunnels, the Norwegians lead the way: the country boasts 1,100 tunnels, 30 of which are under water.

PURE WILDLIFE

The real reason for visiting Norway, though, is the landscape – some regions look as if humans have never set foot there. It's a paradise for nature lovers, with desolate mountains and broad plateaus, home to herds of musk ox, reindeer

1972
Norway votes against joining the European Union

1994
Norway votes against EU membership for the second time

22 July 2011
77 people are killed in a terrorist attack in Oslo and on the island of Utøya. The perpetrator was sentenced to life in prison

2024
Bodø becomes a European Capital of Culture

2025
New vehicles with a petrol or diesel engine can no longer be registered in Norway

and elk. Sea eagles can be spotted encircling the convoluted coastline and sperm whales are attracted by the warm Gulf Stream in the North Sea. In winter, witnessing the Northern Lights is a soul-stirring and exhilarating experience. You can spend weeks hiking through the landscape without meeting a soul. If you

INSIDER TIP
Quench your thirst in nature

want to explore the wildlife and wilderness, it's good to know that nature will not let you starve in Norway: the fjords and rivers offer an abundance of fish, the mountains have a rich supply of clear fresh water and, depending on the season, the countryside is full of mushrooms and berries. However, nature can be unpredictable: warm sunshine can suddenly turn to rain showers and strong winds. While the Gulf Stream keeps the coastal region humid throughout winter, temperatures inland can drop to –40°C. But Norwegians don't let the weather spoil their fun.

TOLERANT AND CALM

Norwegians are often envied for their relaxed and laid-back temperament. How else could they manage to live in a country where it takes over eight hours to drive a distance of 500km? Time is relative; instead of getting hot under the collar, Norwegians respond with a shrug of the shoulders and the matter is forgotten. This behaviour stems from their basic need to live together in harmony. It gives them security and the feeling of living in an open and free society.

Their national holiday on 17 May is when adults act like children for the day and children learn to express their national pride. Many dress up in their national costume, the *bunad*, and sing their national anthem at the top of their lungs at parades and processions: *Ja, vi elsker dette landet* – "Yes, we love this country." The royal family waves from their palace balcony and then there's ice cream for everyone followed by family parties at home in the back garden. They're not only celebrating their independence from Sweden but also the European Union, having voted twice against joining with a polite "thanks, but no thanks", or *nei, takk* in Norwegian.

This national pride has been dinted only once, in 2011 when the far-right extremist Anders Behring Breivik committed an attack on the island of Utøya off the coast of Oslo, killing 77 (mainly young) people. This shooting left the country shocked to its core and united in deep mourning. The prime minister at the time, Jens Stoltenberg, later the Secretary General of NATO, was deeply affected, saying, "We are a small country, but a proud people. We are still shocked by what has happened, but we will never give up our values. Our response is more democracy, more openness, and more humanity. But never naivety."

You can never accuse the Norwegians of being naive; instead, they are quietly proud of having the good fortune to be blessed with affluence, a landscape of stunning beauty and political freedom. Immerse yourself in this land and appreciate its way of life!

AT A GLANCE

5,400,000
inhabitants

Denmark: 5,873,000

96
smartphones
per 100 inhabitants

25,148
kilometres of coastline

UK (including islands): 31,368km

385,203km²
area

UK: 243,610km²

**HIGHEST MOUNTAIN:
GALDHØPPIGEN**

2,469m

Ben Nevis: 1,345m

129
WOLVES

live in the wild in
Norway

**ELECTRIC VEHICLES
REGISTERED IN 2023**

82.4%
UK: 16.5%

FISH ON THE TABLE

Norway's average annual consumption of salmon is 9kg per person

TUNNEL

The Lærdal Tunnel is the longest road
tunnel in the world at 24,509m

97,750km
of public roads
UK: 422,100km

**DEEPEST FJORD
SOGNEFJORD: 1,308m**

UNDERSTAND NORWAY

JUMBO PIGGY BANK

If the national *pensjonsfond* – state pension fund – was paid out today, it would equate to over £232,000 for each of Norway's 5.4 million citizens. A comforting thought that Norwegians like to ponder over now and again. However, instead of cashing them in, the funds, established in 1990 to invest all direct revenues from the oil and gas industry, are saved to secure the prosperity of generations to come. One thing is clear: the vast oil reserves will eventually run dry, and the country's economic mainstay will have to be replaced by alternatives. With or without oil, though, the country's wealth lies at sea. Norway's second most important income stream is salmon, trout and other fish. Unfortunately, though, Norway has long been relying on commercial aquaculture to satisfy the demand for Norwegian fish.

SET IN STONE

The oldest examples of the remaining 28 stave churches are approximately 1,000 years old and are fascinating, especially the Viking carvings which adorn their exteriors: rooftop figures of dragons and snakes winding up the door posts, pagan symbols said to protect Christianity. The buildings' charm lies in the intelligent architecture: made entirely out of wood without any nails or screws, the construction is held up by neatly joined wooden posts and a stone foundation to protect the wooden structure from rotting underneath. The plain and unadorned interior is characterised by remnants of soot, testimony to the countless religious services held inside them. Examples of magnificent and well-preserved stave churches can be seen in Borgund (Lærdal), Heddal (Telemark) and Urnes (Sognefjord).

ROYALS FROM NEXT DOOR

Tall, dark and handsome Crown Prince Haakon is well known for his sporting achievements. In fact, the entire Norwegian Royal House is down to earth, close to its people and, above all, sporty. The crown prince has been known to take part in the Birkebeiner race, a long-distance cross-country ski marathon held annually in Norway. King Harald (now 86) used to be an accomplished yachtsman. Every year the royals turn out to cheer on the ski jumpers at the Ski World Cup in Holmenkollen. Although she may not have won the hearts of the Norwegian people, Crown Princess Mette-Merrit, wife of Crown Prince Haakon and former party girl, has certainly gained their respect. However, her critics accuse her of being snobbish – a claim underpinned by the fact her daughter Ingrid Alexandra attends an exclusive private school in the west of Oslo, usually reserved for children of diplomats, rather than going to the local village school.

BUORRE BEAIVI, OR GOOD DAY!

Red, blue, yellow, green – not a new traffic light system but the traditional colours of the only indigenous people in Europe. The Sami people are characterised by their colourful traditional costumes *(kofta)*, reindeer and *kohte*, or Sami huts, which attract thousands of visitors each year. Their folkloric traditions generate a steady income, but also serve as a reminder of centuries of oppression. Today, the Sami are committed to preserving their language and culture and represent their interests and rights in the Sameting, the advisory assembly in Karasjok. The traditional *joik* is a guttural form of yodelling, and the emotionally driven songs tell stories of ancient times and arduous living conditions in the harsh Nordic climate, of their love of reindeer and their longing for recognition and independence.

Not just for tourists: the Sámi people preserve their culture

THORN IN NORWAY'S SIDE

22 July 2011: This date will be etched in every Norwegian's memory forever as the day when Anders Behring Breivik bombed Oslo's government buildings and then fired indiscriminately at youngsters taking part in a youth camp on the island of Utøya. Seventy-seven people were killed, and Norway showed solidarity in its mourning for the victims, who many knew personally or through friends, by holding up roses as a symbol against intolerance and xenophobia. In June 2022, a memorial site was established directly under the E16 from Oslo to Hønefoss: the 77 narrow bronze statues on the shore draw people into remembrance when looking over at the well-known silhouette of the small island of Utøya.

A BALANCING ACT

Why is it that Scandinavian countries, including Norway, appear to have effortlessly achieved something that other nations have been struggling to get right for years? Their work–life balance is based on the notion that tomorrow is another day, and instead of "living to work", the people of Norway adopt more of a "working to live" attitude. Family and free time take priority. The state endorses this view *and* promotes gender equality: people of all genders are free to

Sky-high entertainment in Kautokeino: the Northern Lights will leave you speechless

decide how they take their (well-paid) parental leave and are guaranteed full-time childcare for their young ones from 18 months onwards. Norway has also established gender equality in its boardrooms – it caused an international stir when it became the first country to enforce a mandatory female quota.

SKY PLAYING TRICKS

The phenomenon known as the Northern Lights, or aurora borealis, makes for a breathtaking display. But be warned, this celestial spectacle carries a health warning, with the potential risks being a stiff neck and a heavy cold. This is because the Northern Lights appear only at high latitudes on cold dark nights from September to March. But they are definitely worth the risk. Stargazers can witness anything from an ethereal green glow or hazy white veil on the horizon to scarlet streaks across the sky. So make yourself a flask of hot tea, put on your warmest clothes and enjoy the experience!

LONG LIVE THE DIALECT

Imagine if pupils in Britain had Dialect on their timetable as a subject alongside English. It may sound unusual, but every Norwegian has to learn both Bokmål, a written language similar to Danish, and Nynorsk, which is based

TRUE OR FALSE?

NEVER WITHOUT A KNITTED JUMPER

It is often said that Norwegians are born with skis on their feet and wearing a warm jumper decorated with a snowflake pattern. That's not quite right: the truth is that Norwegians are stylish dressers, often wearing trendy Scandinavian clothes. Yet it's true that every Norwegian has at least one of the famous jumpers in their wardrobe and likes to wear it during the holidays, at the log cabin or on hikes. So, the classic Norwegian jumper is still a popular garment, especially in cold weather.

on several different dialects. Children have to learn that "How are you?" can be expressed as either *Hvordan har du det?* or *Korleis har du det?* Although you will often hear pupils complaining about the extra work, dialects are an important part of the Norwegian cultural identity and a fully accepted part of everyday life.

THE A-HA EFFECT

The Norwegian soul is a jukebox, serving up all kinds of great music in almost every genre. If you remember the song "Take on me", then you may have been a fan of the boy band A-ha, which enjoyed a string of hits in the 1980s. Since then, others have taken

their place in the pop music charts, including Madcon, Kygo and Nico & Vinz. Röyksopp is an experimental electronic music duo, while Silje Nergaard has made a name for herself with her soft jazz vocals.

BOOKWORMS

When the Norwegians pack their suitcases for the Easter holidays to retreat to their cabins for a week of skiing and relaxation, they are sure to take the latest *påskekrim* (Easter crime fiction) with them. The author Jo Nesbø often releases one of his bestselling crime novels about his Oslo detective Harry Hole just in time for Easter. It's not surprising that Norwegians love a good read: they had to find some way to pass the time during the long winter months before the advent of the internet.

Over the years the country has also produced some of the most prolific writers and dramatists of contemporary social criticism. While Henrik Ibsen is linked to the birth of the modern drama in Europe, Knut Hamsun dedicated his book *Growth of the Soil* to the virtuosity of the farmers and as a result was awarded the Nobel Prize for Literature in 1920. The most influential contemporary Norwegian writer today is Karl Ove Knausgård. His six-volume autobiographical work entitled *My Struggle* was ten years in the making, and the hype surrounding his books is immense: in Norway alone they have sold half a million copies.

SPIRIT OF ADVENTURE

It's a trait probably common among inhabitants of smaller countries, and especially the descendants of the Vikings: Norwegians have an insatiable thirst for knowledge and the curiosity to explore areas beyond their own borders. In the late 19th century, the zoologist and explorer Fridtjof Nansen set out to explore the North Pole on his boat *Fram*. Hard to believe today that the boat, which can be visited on the Oslo museum island of Bygdøy, was trapped in pack ice for over three years. Roald Amundsen has gone down in history as the most successful polar explorer of all time, famous for beating Robert F. Scott in the race to the South Pole. The last in the line of famous Norwegian explorers is Thor Heyerdahl, who built a raft, the *Kon-Tiki*, to cross the Pacific Ocean, proving that

Add nature to your photo album on a boat tour on the Geirangerfjord

people from the Polynesian islands had settled in the Americas.

SET SAIL

If you prefer taking in scenery from the comfort of a deckchair, a cruise is a great way to explore Norway. In 2018, before the coronavirus pandemic, 98 cruise liners docked in the capital Oslo, transporting a total of 200,000 passengers. The most stunning of all the routes is the Hurtigruten (bookings at *hurtigruten.com*). These postal ferry ships have been sailing between Bergen and Kirkenes since 1893, and they not only transport passengers and vehicles but also supply food and provisions to Norway's coastal inhabitants. The ships sail along the rugged west coast and deep into the Geirangerfjord, venturing past the *Seven Sisters Waterfall*, the best views of which can be had from the boat. But not everybody is happy about the environmetal impact of the boom in boats. The Hurtigruten shipping company, however, is leading the way and plans to substantially reduce its seven ships' CO_2 emissions in the coming years.

A GREEN FUTURE

Why do Norwegians always leave the light on? The fact is energy is a readily available and extremely cheap resource in Norway. Almost 99 per cent of all electricity in Norway comes from hydropower thanks to the country's steep mountain slopes and abundance of water. In the past, Norwegians have been accused of being wasteful and complacent about this copious supply, yet in times of

climate change, attitudes are changing and the country has waged a war against the biggest cause of CO_2 pollution – the car. Norway is committed to what many call the "green shift" *(grønn skifte)*, and is often heralded as a pioneer and role model by other countries. For a start, the government has banned diesel cars from driving in Oslo and plans to completely ban the sale of new fossil fuel vehicles by 2025. Norwegian roads are filled with electric cars, and for many drivers the motivation is less about climate protection and more about the financial benefits. Owners of electric cars are rewarded with a wide range of generous tax incentives and perks.

LIGHT NIGHTS

The further north you go, the longer the summer nights are. As soon as you pass into the Arctic Circle, the sun is still shining at midnight. Its light will confuse your body clock. Some people get by with less sleep than usual and feel much fitter for it. However, others get very restless at night, so it's worth packing an eye mask.

BLACK GOLD

Norwegians are passionate about liquorice. It comes in numerous varieties – salty, sweet and spicy, as drops, chews or ice cream. It seems that it's the perfect snack for every occasion. The health authorities have even been known to warn against consuming it in excess, but that doesn't put anyone off buying it. Norwegians love the traditional options, but also get excited when new varieties appear on the shelves!

EATING
SHOPPING
SPORT

Feel-good shopping on Stavanger's "Colourful Street"

EATING & DRINKING

In recent years, Norwegian food has taken off thanks to influences from around the world giving its traditional dishes a refined and international twist.

FROM ALL OVER THE WORLD

There was a time in Norway when the waiter at the local Indian restaurant would ask you, "How would you like your dish – Norwegian, medium or Indian hot?"– "Norwegian" stood for unseasoned and bland. It wasn't long ago that visitors were left feeling uninspired by Norwegian food, surviving off the stalwart pizza with a thick base and plenty of cheese or the traditional *kjøttkaker* or *karbonader* (meat balls) served with boiled potatoes and gravy. Most of it was pretty insipid, and it appeared that garlic and spices had yet to make it across the seas. Norwegians then began to travel further afield and discover a taste for the exotic: alongside Thai, Vietnamese and Indian, sushi has become a firm favourite throughout this country of fish lovers. Norwegian sushi is top-class, second in quality only to Japanese (Japan also happens to be the largest importer of Norwegian fish). It's not surprising, really, when you consider the abundance of fresh fish right on the doorstep. Tacos have replaced pizza as the regular family treat on Fridays. They are easy to make, healthy and children love them.

QUICK DISHES

All sorts of ready meals have become very popular in everyday cooking. The country isn't renowned for its culinary skills, so it may be surprising to learn that some of the best chefs in the world come from Norway. As most Norwegians work full time, elaborate cooking is usually reserved for national holidays or when friends

Mathallen in Oslo offers many delicacies, from preserves to crispbread

come over to visit. Norwegians love to barbecue and will find any excuse to pull out the grill and throw on a *flint-steak*, a gigantic pork chop which could have been named after Fred Flintstone.

Pølse (hotdogs), either in white buns or *lomper* (a soft flatbread made from potato dough) are also readily available at every petrol station or can be thrown onto the barbecue and accompanied with onions, gherkins or a potato salad. Sometimes they are eaten with a prawn salad.

FOR BREAKFAST

Fancy something hearty for breakfast? Why not! Herrings *(sild)*, marinated in a variety of sauces, ranging from tomato, sherry, cream or mustard, are even served at breakfast time. Another classic dish is *makrell i tomat* (mackerel in tomato sauce) – no Norwegian breakfast would be

complete without the iconic yellow tin of Norwegian Stabburet mackerel. Another

INSIDER TIP
Tradition in cans

essential breakfast item is *brunost*, the traditional brown cheese with its unique malty taste. Norwegians like eating it with a thin spreading of jam at the beginning of the day! It can also be packed in a backpack and enjoyed as a snack on a hike in the mountains.

TRADITIONAL CUISINE

Admittedly, traditional Norwegian food isn't to everyone's taste. Although rarely to be found on restaurant menus, a sheep's head *(smalahove)* or cured lamb ribs *(pinnekjøtt)* are traditionally served around Christmas time – the taste reminding you more of the dried twigs that the meat is cooked on than of the meat itself. The consistency of *lutefisk* – dried cod soaked in brine and served with bacon and puréed

A brown cheese called *brunost* makes a tasty breakfast

peas – is somewhat slimy, while *rakørret* (trout soaked in brine for weeks and eaten with onions, cream and potatoes) is definitely worth a try. For a long time the Norwegians' national dish was *fårikål* – a stew of mutton with white cabbage – served especially in autumn. Give it a try!

WHALE OF A TIME

Although the rest of the world (except for Japan) shakes its head disapprovingly at the consumption of whale meat, Norwegians persist in hunting whales. Finely prepared whale carpaccio is considered a delicacy. It's probably best not to enter into discussions on whaling if you're looking for new Norwegian friends. But if you don't want to touch whale meat, but you do want to try something new, you could give reindeer or elk a go: they're very popular with those who like wild meats, enjoyed as a juicy steak or in a burger.

RESTAURANTS

Eating out is expensive in Norway, a luxury to be enjoyed once in a while. Excellent quality wines are available while Nordic beer tends to be on the bland side. Bread, butter and tap water are all served at the table without a surcharge. Norwegians like to finish their meal with a cup of filter coffee, a popular beverage to be drunk at any time of the day. With a per capita consumption of 10kg per year, Norway is topped only by Finland in the world's top coffee-consuming nations. A fatty meal is often digested with a glass of *linie akvavit*. It has been on a long journey across the equator and leaves a warm feeling in your stomach.

Today's Specials

Starters

SPEKETALLERKEN
A selection of smoked hams and
sausages, served with bread

REKESMØR
Prawns and mayonnaise, served with a
fresh salad on white bread

FISKESUPPE
Various types of fish in a creamy soup

DAMPET BLÅSKJELL
Mussels in a white wine sauce, served
with white bread

Main dishes

OVNSBAKT LAKS
Salmon, stuffed with leeks, celeriac and
carrots, baked in the oven and seasoned
with salt and garlic pepper

RØKT ELGSTEIK
Smoked elk meat, braised in the oven,
with root vegetables, Brussels sprouts,
game sauce and boiled potatoes

LAMMESTEIK
Roast lamb seasoned with thyme,
rosemary and garlic

Desserts

EPLEKAKE MED IS
Warm apple cake with cinnamon and
vanilla ice cream

MOLTEKREM
Whipped cream mixed with cloudberry
jam

TROLLKREM
Cranberries mixed with whipped egg
white, served cold

Drinks

GLØGG
Norwegian mulled wine, served with
almonds and raisins

LINIE AKVAVIT
A caraway spirit that has travelled
a long way

SOLBÆRTODDY
Warm currant juice, usually enjoyed
when hiking or skiing

SHOPPING

From wooden toys to ski jackets: you will be spoilt for choice.

SOPHISTICATED DESIGN

Norwegian product designers are full of quirky ideas; a good selection of their modern creations can be found at *Purnorsk* in Oslo or online. How about an oil rig made of wooden building bricks for children? Or a lamp in the shape of a speech bubble from *Northern Lighting*? If you don't have a lot of space in your suitcase, go for one of Norway's best inventions: a steel or silver cheese slicer with a prettily decorated handle.

INSIDER TIP
Cheesy gifts

STAY STYLISH IN THE RAIN

People living in Bergen are used to the rain and time and again come up with ideas for useful all-weather clothing. One such idea is from *Swims*, a take on galoshes that are very popu-lar with business people who want to protect their leather shoes from the rain. Raincoats from *Norwegian Rain* are also fashionable and are even worn when the weather is fine.

IN FASHION

Clothes designed by *Moods of Norway*, the clothing brand with the pink trac-tor logo, have reached almost cult status. Less well known, perhaps, is the eccentric and urban clothing from Oslo designer *Tulip & Tatamo*. The fashionable Crown Princess Mette-Marit swears by fashion from the young label *FWSS (Fall Winter Spring Summer)*.

A CATCH FROM THE FRIDGE

You will be very popular if you bring gourmet delicacies home with you. You can recognise good smoked salmon by its darker colour; it is drier and smells more strongly of smoke

You'll want cold weather for your knitted pullover (photo left) – a great souvenir

than the lower quality fish. Generally speaking, less salt means more taste. Try the salmon before you buy it. Shrink-wrapped salmon from the supermarket can also be good quality, but pay attention to its colour. You can almost taste Norway's rugged coast in a tube of caviar, ideal as a sandwich spread. *Den blinde Ku* (the blind cow), a cheese with a one-eyed cow as its logo, is a cult dairy product and a hit with cheese lovers.

FOR ACTIVE PEOPLE

Outdoor clothing and accessories need to be high quality and sturdy. The Norwegian weather has provided them with a stress test. *Bergans* is a "genuine Norwegian" producer, offering premium quality rucksacks and tents since 1908. The former freestyle skier *Kari Traa* makes universal sportswear for women. *Helly Hansen* is a major name among sailors and yachtsmen. *Odlo* produces fashionable and sustainable ski underwear. *Norrøna* offers brightly coloured ski jackets and trousers, for getting noticed on the slopes.

KNIT TOGETHER

Looking for the quintessential Norwegian souvenir? Then look no further than a traditional pullover – a timeless, high-quality item of clothing available from *Dale of Norway* or *Devold*. Both *Janus* and *Ulvang* specialise in ecological and versatile knitwear. *Nøstebarn* sells cuddly children's clothing made from untreated wool. *Oleana* from Bergen is famous for its beautiful and colourful items of knitwear, inspired by the roses, leaves and vines adorning ancient fishing boats.

SPORT & ACTIVITIES

Norway is an increasingly popular destination for people seeking extreme challenges. But it also has plenty to offer anyone who just wants to get out there and be active.

Coasts and fjords, fantastic rivers, and lakes at all elevations are perfect for anglers and water sport enthusiasts, while the mountains offer challenges to hikers and mountaineers. And, of course, winter sports naturally take centre stage.

ANGLING
Norway is a paradise for anglers and, thanks to its never-ending coastline, it's especially popular with those who love to fish in the sea. Every inhabited island and coastal town has areas that cater especially to fishing enthusiasts. Angling in the sea and fjords is free, but sport fishing in rivers and lakes requires permission from the lease-holder *(contact the Tourist Information*

Office for more details). If you aim to catch salmon and sea trout, you also need to pay a fishing fee *(fiskeravgift | 286 NOK)*. This can be done ahead of time online *(fiskeravgift.miljo direktoratet.no)*. You should also pay attention to the export regulations (see Customs information on p. 137).

CYCLING
You can explore Norway by bike. Bikes can be hired directly at the start of the most popular cycling routes or at the airports *(Fly & Bike)*. A less-strenuous option is to hire an electric bike, available in *Hammerfest (firmapost@ gagama.no)* for guided tours. The challenging *Rallarvegen* between Oslo and Bergen takes cyclists through the wild and rugged Hardangervidda National Park. The *Jæren* region, which starts in *Stavanger*, is more suitable for children. A 450km cycling route starts in *Andenes*, at the

An icy adventure: a canoe tour of the lake at Jostedalsbreen glacier

northern tip of Vesterålen, and runs to Å, the most southerly point of the Lofoten Islands. Off-road bikers can hire bikes and equipment from the *Hafjell Bikepark (hafjell.no)*. You can find all the bike trails with a handy guide at *cycletourer.co.uk*.

DIVING

If you have the right equipment, diving in the fjords and along the coast is an unforgettable experience that is attracting more and more people. The organised dive in the world's strongest tidal current, *Saltstraumen* near Bodø, is exceptional. Wreck diving around the *Frankenwald* ship that sank in 1940 at the Sognefjord is a wonderful, haunting experience. And, of course, the coral reefs, such as the ones at *Hottane* (Møre og Romsdal), offer a lot to see, including countless fish, crabs and lobsters. Those seeking an adrenalin rush can go for a night dive at *Tysfjord* and may, with a bit of luck, meet the orcas there.

EXTREME SPORTS

Ice climbing in *Hemsedal*, rafting on the raging *Trysilelva River*, wreck diving in *Vestland*, ski-mountaineering over the *Hardangervidda* – the Norwegian landscape offers countless sporting activities in summer and winter that will push your body to its limits. Beginners can also take part safely and are assisted by experienced instructors who make sure the emphasis is on fun.

More experienced athletes should attempt the *Birkebeiner (birkebeiner. no)* with like-minded adrenalin junkies. Whether you choose the cross-country skiing (54km), cycling (100km) or cross-country running (21km) races, the aim is to get your pulse racing in Norway's rugged nature and unpredictable weather.

GOLF

Only true golf addicts will take their clubs to Norway. The country offers the chance to play on some of the world's most unusual golf courses. *Meland* near Bergen is regarded as the most challenging of all. The world's most northerly course, the *Tromsø Golf Park*, is very picturesque, but probably the most beautiful of all is the *Lofoten Golfbane (lofoten-golf.no)*, located directly next to the open sea. You can play on the green until late in the evening in summer under the light of the midnight sun. *Norges Golfforbund (tel. 21 02 91 50 | golfforbundet.no)*

HIKING & CLIMBING

Space and seclusion can be found all over Norway. The well-marked trails and basic to comfortable cabins make the high plateaus, mountains and islands attractive destinations.

Backpackers are especially fond of the *Saltfjellet-Svartisen* and *Øvre Pasvik* national parks in northern Norway, *Bjørgefjell* and *Dovrefjell-Sunndalsfjella* in the centre of the country, *Jotunheimen* and *Rondane* in the south – and, of course, the *Hardangervidda*. The cabins are usually located three to eight hours' walk from each other. You can obtain detailed information from the Norwegian Hiking Association *DNT (Oslo | tel. 40 00 18 70 | dnt.no)*. Almost all the *DNT* routes are described briefly at *ut.no*.

DNT also provides essential information for climbers and mountaineers. The most popular areas for these activities are the demanding peaks in the west of *Jotunheimen* and around *Jostedalsbreen* glacier. Glacier hikes with experienced guides are offered there, as well as at *Folgefonna* glacier *(tel. 95 11 77 92 | folgefonni.no)* near Hardangerfjord, throughout the summer. *Nordfjord Aktiv (tel. 90 08 91 70 | nordfjordaktiv.no)* in the western region of Nordfjord is a very good outfit (for mountain-bike tours as well). Local mountaineering clubs can be contacted through the tourist information offices.

SAILING & RAFTING

The entire south coast from Oslo to Egersund is a superb *sailing* area but it often gets quite crowded in the harbours. However, you will always find a calm bay where you can drop anchor. The harbours to the north are more sheltered and also have more room.

Canoeing and kayaking are more typically Norwegian than sailing: offers range from tours along the coast and in the fjords to trips from lake to lake (take a tent and sturdy shoes) and whitewater rafting on one of the rivers that flow from the alpine regions to the east or west. The number one place for this is the *Sjoa*, a tributary of the Lågen in the upper Gudbrandsdalen region. There are half-, one- or two-day tours. You can get information from *Sjoa Rafting (Nedre Heidal | tel. 90 07 10 00 | sjoarafting. no)*. You will get a taste of the Arctic, freedom and adventure on a kayak tour on the glacial lakes at Jostedalsbreen *(organised by Icetroll | Breheimsenteret Jostedal | tel. 97 01 43 70 | icetroll.com)*.

INSIDER TIP
Ice-cold paddling

SKIING

In a country with so much space, there are an infinite number of cross-country trails. They begin in front of your house or cabin door, are often floodlit, and can run for dozens of kilometres. And, you can be sure of there being snow from November to April – at least east of the fjords and from Nordland to the North Cape.

Alpine skiers have also discovered Norway, and they can choose from a handful of first-class destinations. *Trysilfjellet (skistar.com/trysil)* near the Swedish border is ideal for families, as is the Olympic town of *Lillehammer*. *Geilo (geilo.no)*, between Oslo and Bergen, offers the best combination of alpine and cross-county skiing. Young alpinists who are into off-piste skiing travel to *Stranda (strandafjellet.no)* near Ålesund or Hemsedal *(hemsedal.com)*.

Barren rock and plenty of fresh air in the Jotunheimen National Park

REGIONAL OVERVIEW

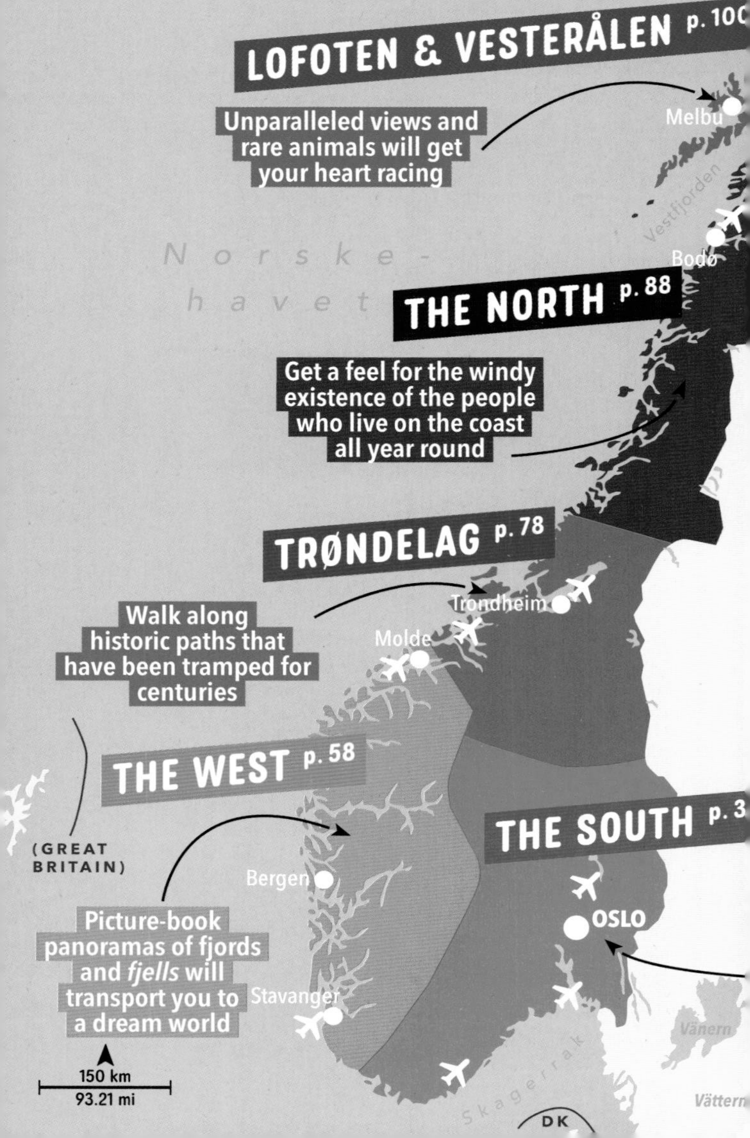

LOFOTEN & VESTERÅLEN p. 100

Unparalleled views and rare animals will get your heart racing

Melbu

Vestfjorden

Bodø

Norske-
havet

THE NORTH p. 88

Get a feel for the windy existence of the people who live on the coast all year round

TRØNDELAG p. 78

Walk along historic paths that have been tramped for centuries

Trondheim

Molde

THE WEST p. 58

(GREAT
BRITAIN)

Picture-book panoramas of fjords and *fjells* will transport you to a dream world

Bergen

Stavanger

THE SOUTH p. 3

OSLO

Vänern

150 km
93.21 mi

Skagerrak

DK

Vättern

Hammerfest

Varangerfjorden

FINNMARK p. 118

Inarijärvi

**Discover the ways of
the Sami people**

Tromsø

TROMS p. 110

Narvik

**Explore the "end of the
world" with Arctic air in
your lungs**

Storavan

SWEDEN

FINLAND

Ladožskoe
ozero

Selkämeri
Bottenhavet

njoy the cool air in the
space between town
and country

ESTONIA

Čudskoe
ozero

LATVIA

THE SOUTH

URBAN CENTRES AND RUGGED LANDSCAPES

The South has everything. Hip cities and exciting architecture give it its typical Norwegian character of modernity and originality, but these are coupled with deserted landscapes with spectacular views of fjords, coastlines and secret forests.

The landscape of the southern coastline has also shaped its inhabitants: they are cool, at one with nature, and traditional; they are grounded and relaxed, and not at all uptight. It's no surprise when

Expansive sky and plenty of fresh air: the mountainous Jotunheimen region

you consider they spend every free minute surrounded by breathtaking landscapes. They pack up their hiking backpack, skis or swimming kit, depending on the time of year and the weather, and set off to find deserted mountain lakes, fish for sea trout, or dive into the 20°C waves of the Skagerrak strait off sandy beaches, as if they were in southern Europe. Southern Norway is ideal for anyone who wants to slow down but still experience lively cities.

THE SOUTH

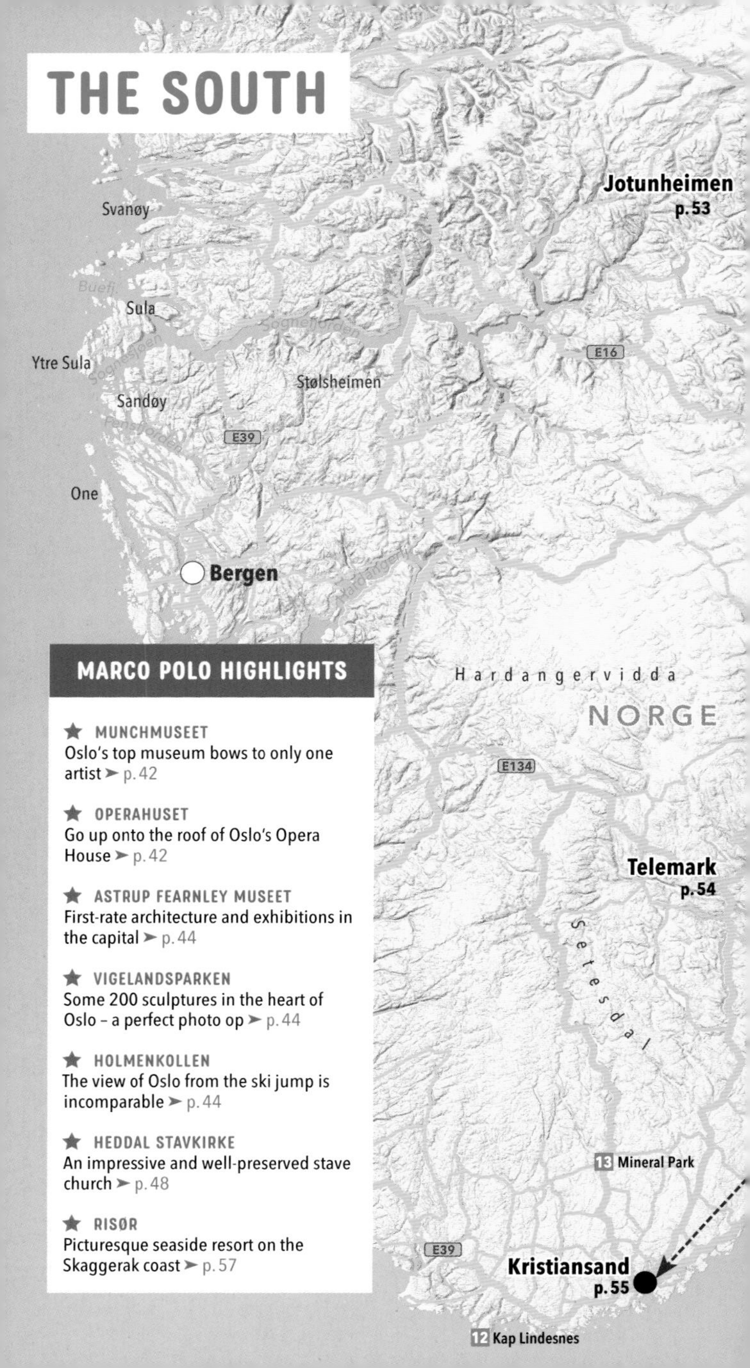
Svanøy
Sula
Ytre Sula
Sandøy
Stølsheimen
E39
One
Bergen
Jotunheimen
p. 53
E16
Hardangervidda
NORGE
E134
Telemark
p. 54
Setesdal
13 Mineral Park
E39
Kristiansand
p. 55
12 Kap Lindesnes

MARCO POLO HIGHLIGHTS

★ **MUNCHMUSEET**
Oslo's top museum bows to only one artist ➤ p. 42

★ **OPERAHUSET**
Go up onto the roof of Oslo's Opera House ➤ p. 42

★ **ASTRUP FEARNLEY MUSEET**
First-rate architecture and exhibitions in the capital ➤ p. 44

★ **VIGELANDSPARKEN**
Some 200 sculptures in the heart of Oslo – a perfect photo op ➤ p. 44

★ **HOLMENKOLLEN**
The view of Oslo from the ski jump is incomparable ➤ p. 44

★ **HEDDAL STAVKIRKE**
An impressive and well-preserved stave church ➤ p. 48

★ **RISØR**
Picturesque seaside resort on the Skaggerak coast ➤ p. 57

OSLO

(□ D16) **A small capital city with a vast hinterland: Norway's metropolis (pop. 680,000) at the foot of the Oslofjord climbs up the slopes of the wooded Nordmarka region.**

Oslo first became the seat of the Norwegian royal family under King Håkon V (1299–1319). The town was called Christiania from the 14th to the beginning of the 19th century, when Norway was still part of Denmark, and it was overshadowed by Copenhagen, Bergen and Trondheim. It only started to flourish again at the end of the 19th century and in 1925 it was given its old name once more.

You should definitely visit the historic district of Oslo near Akershus Fortress. The "citizen's quarter" near Frognerparken and the multicultural Grønland suburb to the east of the main station are also well worth seeing. Oslo's smart shopping street, Karl Johans gate, stretches from the railway station to the Royal Palace – the palace square offers one of the prettiest views in the city. With the *Oslo Pass (24 hrs 445 NOK, 48 hrs 665 NOK, 72 hrs 820 NOK | visitoslo.com)* you can travel by bus and train and visit most of the main sights.

More detailed information can be found in the Marco Polo travel guide for Oslo.

WHERE TO START?

Operahuset *(□ f5)*: The Opera House is the perfect starting point for a stroll around Oslo as it is located directly between the fjord and the main station. Drive to one of the many multistorey car parks near the railway station, walk across to the Opera House, make your way up to its rooftop and start planning your stroll through the city.

SIGHTSEEING

MUNCHMUSEET ★

The building has a bend in it, as if it were bowing to Norway's most famous artist, Edvard Munch. It's the only museum of its size in the world created for just one artist. There are 13 floors with around 1,100 paintings, 15,500 graphic works and 4,700 drawings, as well as cafés, restaurants, concert halls and artists' studios. Munch's world-famous painting *The Scream*, which is obviously featured here, has competition: the breathtaking view from the *Skybar* on the 13th floor. *Mon–Wed 10am–6pm, Thu–Sun 10am–9pm | admission 160 NOK, Thu 6–9pm free | Munchbrygge | munchmuseet.no | ⊙ 2 hrs | □ f6*

OPERAHUSET ★

The award-winning opera house on Bjørvika Bay is an Oslo landmark: white marble, lots of glass, a magnificent interior and a roof with a panoramic view, open to the public – a wonderful experience whatever the weather. *Tours in English Mon–Sat 1pm, Sun 2pm | admission 120 NOK | operaen.no | ⊙ 1 hr | □ f5*

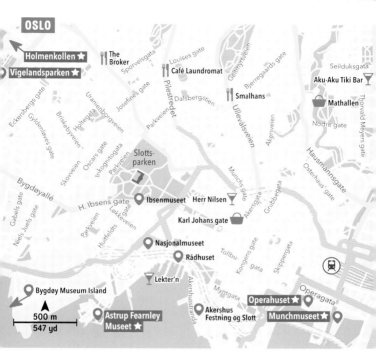

OSLO

Holmenkollen ★
Vigelandsparken ★
The Broker
Café Laundromat
Smalhans
Aku-Aku Tiki Bar
Mathallen
Ibsenmuseet
Herr Nilsen
Karl Johans gate
Nasjonalmuseet
Rådhuset
Lekter'n
Bygdøy Museum Island
500 m
547 yd
Astrup Fearnley Museet ★
Akershus Festning og Slott
Operahuset ★
Munchmuseet ★

AKERSHUS FESTNING OG SLOTT

One of the most important medieval buildings in Norway sits on a promontory jutting out into the Oslofjord. Akershus was a fortress from 1319 to 1380 and was transformed into a *castle* by King Christian IV at the beginning of the 17th century. Today, it is used for state receptions while the 🐦 fortress complex is a favourite place for sun worshippers. *Fortress complex daily 6am–9pm | free admission | castle May–Aug Mon–Sat 10am–4pm, Sun noon–4pm, otherwise Sat/Sun noon–5pm | admission 100 NOK | FB: akershus slott | ⏱ 45 mins | ▦ d–e 5–6*

RÅDHUSET 🐦

With its two towers, the red-brick town hall, built between 1930 and 1955, stands like a mighty gate between the harbour and inner city. Inside, you can see impressive monumental paintings, including works by Edvard Munch. *Daily 9am–4pm | free admission | ⏱ 45 mins | ▦ d4*

NASJONALMUSEET

The National Museum – opened in 2022 – is next door to the Nobel Peace Centre at the town hall square and provides Oslo with a giant stamp of artistic excellence: it exhibits over 6,500 works across 80 exhibition rooms and has a total surface area of

54,600m². The art includes paintings, sculptures, design artefacts and installations, making it a new meeting point for the city. *Tue–Sun 10am–9pm | admission 180 NOK | Brynjulf Bulls plass 3 | nasjonalmuseet.no | ⏱ 2 hrs | 🗺 d4*

ASTRUP FEARNLEY MUSEET ⭐

Oslo's architectural masterpiece is situated directly on the fjord. The collection of this museum on the Tjuvholmen promontory includes works by Damien Hirst, Andy Warhol, Jeff Koons and Anselm Kiefer. A stroll through the steel-and-glass buildings designed by Renzo Piano topped by a "sail" is an experience in itself, and the temporary exhibits are excellent. *Tue–Fri noon–5pm (Thu until 7pm), Sat/Sun 11am–5pm | admission 150 NOK | Strandpromenaden 2 | afmuseet.no | ⏱ 2 hrs | 🗺 c5*

IBSENMUSEET

"Eternally owned is but what's lost" is just one of 69 quotes embedded in the pavement where Henrik Ibsen, the most famous Norwegian writer, once walked every day. He's the founder of modern drama and one of the most important names in Realism. He's still one of the world's most performed authors today. The trail of quotes starts at his apartment in Arbins gate, today the *Ibsen Theatre. (At the time of publishing, this site is closed for renovation until further notice) Henrik Ibsens gate 26 | ibsenmuseet.no | 🗺 c4*

VIGELANDSPARKEN ⭐ 🐗

The complex with around 200 sculptures by Gustav Vigeland is just one section of the vast Frognerparken that is especially popular in summer. You should take your time walking up the avenue of stones leading to the 17m-high *Monolitten* and take in the aura of the figures that depict the cycle of life. From the upper end, you have a great view over the park and suburb of Frogner all the way to the city centre. *Open 24 hrs daily | free admission | main entrance Kirkeveien | vigelandmuseum.no | ⏱ 1 hr | 🗺 a1–2*

HOLMENKOLLEN ⭐ 🚩

The "mecca for Norwegian skiers" is dominated by the extremely modern main ski jump. The view of the city, the fjord and the surrounding forests is breathtaking. If you come here, you should also visit the *Ski Museum. May–Sept daily 10am–5pm, otherwise 10am–4pm | admission 160 NOK | holmenkollen.com | 8km northwest of the city centre | T-Bane line 1 from Majorstuen station | ⏱ 1 hr | 🗺 0*

BYGDØY MUSEUM ISLAND

The ideal destination to get your first impressions of Norway's history and culture. The *Fram-Museet (June–Aug daily 10am–6pm, otherwise shorter opening hours | admission 140 NOK | frammuseum.no)* is devoted to a single ship. Built in 1892, the three-masted *Fram* (Forwards) was the expedition ship in which Fridtjof Nansen, Otto Sverdrup and Roald Amundsen set sail for the Arctic and Antarctic. You can see the adventurer

Exciting architecture at the Astrup Fearnley Museet

and researcher Thor Heyerdahl's *Kon-Tiki* raft, the papyrus boat *Ra II* and a model of the *Tigris* in the *Kon-Tiki-Museum (June–Aug daily 10am–6pm, otherwise shorter opening times | admission 140 NOK | kon-tiki.no)*.

Gjøa, the yacht Roald Amundsen used to sail around North America between 1903 and 1905 belongs to the collection of the *Norsk Maritimt Museum (mid-May–Sept daily 10am–5pm, otherwise shorter opening hours | admission 140 NOK | marmuseum.no)*. The *Vikingskipshuset* is closed until 2026/27 for renovations.

One hundred and seventy houses have been rebuilt in the *Norsk Folkemuseum (May–Sept daily 10am–5pm, otherwise shorter opening times | admission 180 NOK | norskfolke museum.no)* to show what life in

Norway has been like over the centuries. The oldest building is the stave church of Gol (c. 1200). ⏲ *3 hrs |* 🕮 *a6*

EATING & DRINKING

CAFÉ LAUNDROMAT

At Café Laundromat you can do your laundry while enjoying a Lucky Bastard (don't worry, it's just a burger!). Breakfast is served until 5pm. Close to the university, with a living room setting. *Underhaugsveien 2 | tel. 21 38 36 29 | laundromat.no | ££ |* 🕮 *d2*

> **INSIDER TIP**
> Home from home

SMALHANS

Casual atmosphere with a concept to match its clientele. Order lunch at the bar (until 4pm) and put together your own menu at your table after 6pm. A dish of the day is offered in between. *Waldemar Ullevålsveien 43 | tel. 22 69 60 00 | smalhans.no | £££ | 🕮 e2*

THE BROKER
Best burgers in town and perfectly poured beer. *Bogstadveien 27 | online reservations | thebroker.no | £ | 🕮 c1*

SHOPPING

KARL JOHANS GATE
Stroll through the pedestrian zone that has every international brand you can think of. For more relaxed shopping, head to *Steen & Strøm (Nedre Slottsgate, adjacent to Karl Johans gate)* and *Paleet (Karl Johans gate 37).* 🕮 d–e4

MATHALLEN
A temple for the gourmet, with organic products from all over Norway, ranging from seafood delicacies to sausages and cheese. It includes small stands and shops, restaurants, bistros and snack bars. *Closed Mon | Vulkan 5 | 🕮 f2*

SPORT & ACTIVITIES

Get out of the city and you'll soon find yourself immersed in the rugged wilderness of *Nordmarka (🕮 0).* The forests, mountains and countless small lakes are popular with Oslo residents out for an excursion, even in the wind and rain. This recreation area starts at the Holmenkollen Ski Centre and offers 2,600km of prepared cross-country trails. Skiers and hikers

Big-city flair at Oslo's Karl Johans Gate, running from the train station to the castle

can either stay overnight in cabins or just come for the day.

WELLNESS

THE WELL

This stylish spa oasis offers everything you need for a day of wellness. What

INSIDER TIP
Relax in the forest

do you want to treat yourself to first? A hamam or a waterfall grotto? Once you're here, you'll never want to leave. *Kongeveien 65 | Sofiemyr | 15km/ 25 mins by bus from Oslo S to stop Granholtet | tel. 48 04 48 88 | thewell. no | ▥ 0*

NIGHTLIFE

AKU-AKU TIKI BAR

INSIDER TIP
Aloha!

Here you can drink tasty cocktails while watching hula dancers perform. *Thorvald Meyers gate 32 | akuaku.no | ▥ f2*

HERR NILSEN

The daily concerts have something for all jazz fans – simply turn up and enjoy the surprise. *C J Hambros Plass 5 | herrnilsen.no | ▥ e4*

LEKTER'N

What could be nicer than taking a walk along Aker Brygge and finding yourself drinking a gin and tonic at a boat-bar directly on the water? Give it a go. The sunset is spectacular from here. *Stranden 3 | lektern.no | ▥ c5*

AROUND OSLO

▣ DRØBAK

36km / 30 mins from Oslo (by bus: line 500 from Oslo bus terminals)
If you want to feel Christmassy, you should go to Drøbak. The beautifully preserved town has a range of cafés to choose from and numerous shops selling crafts. In *Tregaarden's Julehus*

INSIDER TIP
Christmas all year!

(Havnebakken 6 | jule hus.no), you can buy Christmas decorations all year round. If you walk by *Guri Malla Is og Spiseri (Torget 3 | FB: gurimallaisogkaffe.no),* you will get hungry just looking at the sandwiches. *▥ C17*

▢ TJØME

124km / 1 hr 40 mins from Oslo (by car via E18)
This narrow island that juts into the Skagerrak strait on the western side of Oslofjord is joined to the mainland by a bridge and is a popular destination for sun worshippers and gourmets. The famous guesthouse *Engø Gård (Gamlke Engø vei 25 | tel. 33 39 00 48 | engo.no | £££)* is located in a magnificent natural park. Those who just want to explore the island may well find themselves at *Verdens Ende* – the end of the world. The southern tip is easy to spot thanks to the historic lighthouse from 1932. Its mighty rock is the perfect place for couples to stroll on a summer's evening. *▥ D–E17*

Why not take a journey (through time) to Fredrikstad?

3 KONGSBERG

86km / 1½ hrs from Oslo (by car via E18 and E134)

The mining town (pop. 27,000) was founded in 1624 after silver was discovered there. In 1770, almost 10,000 people lived in the town; 4,000 of them worked in the silver mines, including many miners from other parts of Europe. A trip on the 2.3km-long pit railway of the 🌲 *Norwegian Mining Museum (mid-May–mid-Aug several departure times daily | 250 NOK | norskbergverksmuseum.no)*, followed by a one-hour tour of the mine tunnels, is a unique experience. ⊞ C16

4 HEDDAL STAVKIRKE ★

122km / 2 hrs from Oslo (by car via E18 and E134)

Norway's largest stave church is located right on the E134 near Notodden. It was built around 1200, has three naves and is notable for its overlapping roofs and intricately carved porch with animal ornaments. The interior is richly decorated, including fine rose paintings. *June–Aug Mon–Sat 10am–5pm, Sun after service from 12.15pm | admission 90 NOK | heddalstavkirke.no | ⏱ 45 mins | ⊞ C17*

5 BJØRNEPARKEN 🎭

120km / 2 hrs from Oslo (by car via E16)

Forests and lakes lead to the heart of the park, where you can watch bears, moose and many other animals in a natural-style compound. *Early April–Oct daily 10am–4pm | admission from 18 June adult 459 NOK, child 419 NOK, otherwise 399 and 369 NOK | bjorneparken.no | ⏱ 2½ hrs | ⊞ C16*

FREDRIKSTAD

(☐ D17) **Once you arrive, you'll never want to leave! Situated in the far south of Norway and 40km from the Swedish border, a visit to the idyllic town of Fredrikstad is like stepping back in time.**

The town's pretty and historic charm is captivating. The former garrison town (pop. 84,000) remains an insider tip among tourists and the surrounding region also has plenty to offer: Norway's longest river, the Glomma, flows into the town from the northeast and merges into the Oslofjord upon leaving the city.

SIGHTSEEING

FREDRIKSTAD DOMKIRKE (CATHEDRAL)

The best time to visit this neo-Gothic church dating from 1880 is at night: the steeple contains a lighthouse, which you wouldn't necessarily notice in the daytime. Those visiting by day should go inside to admire the stained-glass work by Emanuel Vigeland. *Mon–Fri 10am–2pm | Nygaardsgata 6 | ⊙ 20 mins*

GAMLEBYEN (FORT & OLD TOWN)

Since it was founded in 1567, the old town has lost little of its charm. Take time to wander through the many galleries and art and craft shops. Small restaurants and coffee shops, such as *Café Magenta* at Bastion 5, serve refreshments – try traditional smoked salmon on bread with scrambled egg.

FREDRIKSTAD MUSEUM

It is not clear where the museum stops and *Bar 1567* begins – making this museum all the more interesting. Take a trip back through the history of Fredrikstad accompanied by music, theatre and dance and explore a different side to this charming town. *June–Sept daily 11am–4pm, otherwise shorter opening times | admission 90 NOK | Tøihusgaten 41 | ostfold museene.no | ⊙ 1 hr*

EATING & DRINKING

MAJOREN STUE & KRO

Travel back to garrison times: the authentic *majorens viltburger* fits perfectly with the historic ambience. *Voldportgaten 73 | tel. 69 32 15 55 | majoren.no | £££*

MORMORS CAFÉ

Organic dishes are made to order at this café/restaurant in the old town centre. Their fresh bread is perfect for the tasty delicacies such as the roast beef sandwich with truffle aioli and parmesan cheese. *Raadhusgaten 18A | tel. 69 32 16 60 | mormorscafe.com | ££*

SHOPPING

GLASSHYTTA

A touch of Africa: the products made by Kenyan glass artist Abel Sawe are characterised by their strong colours and unusual forms. *Torsnesveien 1 | fredrikstad oghvaler.no/glasshytta*

AROUND FREDRIKSTAD

6 HVALER

22km / 30 mins from Fredrikstad (by car via Fylkesvei 108)

An island-hopping adventure. The municipality of Hvaler is a group of 833 islands, holms and islets. You can explore this picture-book region by taking a boat trip with *Hvaler ferries (70 NOK | tel. 90 85 71 21 | ostfold-kollektiv.no)*, which docks at several picturesque beaches along the way, including Kirkeøy in the far south. The tour starts in the main centre of Skjærhalden. In *Café Oline (July/Aug daily from noon | Søndre Sandøy | tel. 48 32 66 66)*, imagine you're in your grand-ma's garden, looking out over the sea with fresh prawns on your plate.

INSIDER TIP
Idyllic coastal gardens

LILLE HAMMER

(⊞ D15) **Have you ever dreamt of how it felt to be a ski jumper at the 1994 Winter Olympics?**

In Lillehammer (pop. 28,000), you can head straight to the ski-jumping centre *Lysgårdsbakken (June–Aug daily 11am–6pm, otherwise shorter opening times | admission 25 NOK | Birkebeinervegen 122 | olympia-parken.no)*. From the top of the ski jump, you have amazing panoramic views of the town over to the Mjøsa Lake, Norway's largest inland lake. If you're not prepared to walk up the 936 steps to get there, the chairlift will take you up and down for 60 NOK.

SIGHTSEEING

NORGES OLYMPISKE MUSEUM

This museum is dedicated to Norway's main national sport. If you share the Norwegians' passion for skiing, you are sure to love this homage to the legendary Winter Olympics held in Norway in 1952 and 1994. With cheering crowds and glorious winners, the multimedia presentations are sure to set your pulse racing. *June–Aug daily 10am–5pm, otherwise Tue–Sun 11am–4pm | admission 140 NOK | Maihaugvegen 1 | ol.museum. no | ⊙ 1 hr*

MAIHAUGEN

Lillehammer is the gateway to Gudbrandsdalen. More than 170 buildings will not only give you an idea of the rural culture of the valley but also of the handicrafts from all over Norway. Many of the workshops are still in use. Changing exhibitions. 🐾 Children from six years old can practise their skills on the balance course. *June–Aug daily 10am–5pm, otherwise shorter open-ing times | admission 140 NOK, children and young people (6–25 years old) 65 NOK | Maihaugvegen 1 | maihaugen.no | ⊙ 2½ hrs*

INSIDER TIP
Balancing ac

Maihaugen open-air museum: life in Gudbrandsdalen in days gone by

EATING & DRINKING

DET LILLE PANNEKAKEHUS

Sweet dishes of blueberries and ice cream, savoury dishes of bacon and cheese: enjoy the best of both worlds. The pancakes and Dutch *poffertjes* are divine. *Storgata 50*

INSIDER TIP
Mmmmh ...

NIKKERS RESTAURANT & BAR

Enjoy traditional Norwegian food – smoked salmon on bread, moose burger – with a modern twist. In summer, you can sit on the terrace right on the River Mesna. *Elvegata 18 | tel. 61 24 74 30 | nikkers.no | ££*

SHOPPING

JANUS FABRIKKBUTIKK

Traditional ski underwear from Janus comes from Espeland near Bergen.

This store is one of four factory outlets. These cosy fleece garments keep you so warm that you'll want to take a set back home. *Storgata 45 | tel. 47 61 38 00 00 | janus.no*

AROUND LILLEHAMMER

7 HAMAR

60km / 1 hr from Lillehammer (by car via E6)

Surprisingly, Hamar (pop. 32,000) is the place to visit on rainy days because the ☂ *ruins of the cathedral* and the partially excavated *bishop's palace* are preserved under a gigantic glass pyramid and you can stay dry while learning more about this former religious centre in Norway. You'll need better weather, though, if you're going to explore the 65 buildings in the *Hedmark outdoor museum* next door and to enjoy a picnic on the banks of the delightful Mjøsa Lake. *Late June–mid-Aug daily 10am–5pm, otherwise shorter opening times | admission to ruins and museum 140 NOK | Strandvegen 100 | dom-kirkeodden.no | ⊙ 1 hr (for ruins and museum) | ▭ D15*

children (90–119cm) from 359 NOK | It's easier to buy tickets in advance online | Fossekrovegen 22 | Fåberg | hunderfossen.no | ⊙ 3 hrs | ▭ D15

9 AULESTAD

18km / 20 mins from Lillehammer (by car via Fylkesvei 255)
Blueberry pancakes were the favourite food of the Norwegian national poet

Return to nature: walking in Rondane National Park

8 HUNDERFOSSEN EVENTYRPARK 🎭

16km / 20 mins from Lillehammer (by car via E 6)
A 14m-high troll lives in this adventure park alongside a fairytale castle, a house of wax figures, paths and a pool. The energy centre provides a lot of information, mostly about hydro-electric energy. *Mid-June–mid-Aug daily 10am–6pm, otherwise 10am–5pm | admission from 411 NOK,*

Bjørnstjerne Bjørnson. It's worth taking a detour to his residence if only to enjoy its idyllic setting: time seems to have stood still in 1875 and the *Drengestua* (servants' quarters) café serves delicious pancakes. *June–Aug daily 10am–5pm, otherwise shorter opening times | admission 140 NOK | Aulestadvegen 6am–2pm | Follebu | aulestad.no | ⊙ 1½ hrs | ▭ D15*

10 PEER GYNT VEGEN

45km / 45 mins from Lillehammer to Skeikampen (by car via E 6)

This splendid mountain road is over 60km long and takes you to heights of more than 1,000m. Take a break along the way to soak up the magnificent view of the Jotunheimen, Rondane and Dovrefjell mountains. Elks can be spotted here until well into autumn (guided safari tours in Gålå) and you can spend hours fishing for freshwater trout, hiking through this beautiful region and enjoying a break at the *Fagerhøy Alm (fagerhoi.no)*. The road also attracts cyclists. The *Peer Gynt Festival (tickets from 745 NOK | peergynt.no)* takes place here every year at the start of August. Henrik Ibsen's famous play is performed, accompanied by the music composed by Edvard Grieg. *Toll station (150 NOK one way) | peergyntvegen.no |* *C–D 14–15*

11 RONDANE NATIONAL PARK

120km / 1 hr 40 mins from Lillehammer to Mysuseter Servicesenter (by car via E6)

"Back to nature" is the motto in this 964km² national park, which also welcomes camper vans. Standing an impressive 10m high, the world's largest elk sculpture greets drivers at the parking area at *Bjøråa* if you take a detour via the E3 when travelling south. Stretching out over Gudbrandsdalen, Dovrefjell, Jotunheimen and Rondane, the region is home to Norway's highest mountains, making it a paradise for recreational pursuits including hiking, fishing, rafting and ski mountaineering. What's more, you can relax with a spot of animal watching or a massage for aching muscles at the spa in the *Rondane Høyfjellshotell (turn off the E6 at Otta | tel. 61 20 90 90 | rondane.no). nasjonalparkriket.no |* *C–D14*

JOTUNHEIMEN

(C14) **Translated literally, Jotunheimen means "homeland of the giants". It is Norway's only high mountain range, making it a popular destination for hikers, mountaineers and skiers.**

Here, a chain of mountains over 2,000m high stretches out, one peak after the other, many of them crowned with glaciers. However, even the highest of them, Galdhøpiggen – at 2,469m the highest mountain in all of Scandinavia – can be climbed by children.

SIGHTSEEING

NORSK FJELLSENTER

A good place for tourist tips. In the museum next door, discover how this barren region with its harsh winters and short summers has affected the lives of its inhabitants. *Mid-May–late June and mid-Aug–mid-Oct Mon–Fri 10am–4pm, late June–mid-Aug 9am–7pm | admission 130 NOK | Brubakken 2 | Lom | norskfjellsenter.no | 45 mins*

GALDHØPIGGEN

Norway's highest peak is accessible even for children and dogs. All you need is good waterproof outdoor clothing (and a sturdy dog that can withstand a storm or hailstones), as the weather can be extremely variable. The 15km guided tour *(May–Oct daily from 10am | 380 NOK | starts from Juvasshytta)* will take you there and back in six to seven hours.

KLIMAPARK 2469

INSIDER TIP
Icy pleasures

Nobody will laugh at you for wearing a hat and gloves here in the middle of summer. On the contrary, you'll be well pre-pared to go into the solid ice beneath you. The guided tour takes you on a hike through the climate park fol-lowed by a 400m-long ice tunnel underneath Galdhøpiggen Mountain. The ice cave also contains bows and arrows, pitfalls and tools of the first cave inhabitants and tracks the cli-mate changes over the last 6,000 years. *Guided tours (best to book online) mid-June–late August, 10.30am–2pm from the Juvasshytta mountain hut | 375 NOK (including admission to Norsk Fjellsenter) | klimapark2469.no | ⏱ 2½ hrs*

SOGNEFJELLSVEI

Road 55 from Lom to Skjolden is a landscaped scenic route that runs through icy heights. With a place to stop for a rest at 1,400m, glacier snouts, hiking trails and places to fish to the left and right of the road, the journey to Skjolden is an eventful

encounter with Norway's mountain world. *short.travel/nor16*

EATING & DRINKING

BAKERIET I LOM

Master chef Morten Schakenda decided to become a baker and opened a bakery and slow-food café at the Prestefosse waterfall in Lom – it's a joy for all the senses. Make sure you try the cinnamon rings. *bakerietilom.no*

INSIDER TIP
Lead with your nose

TELEMARK

(▢ B–C 16–17) **It is considered the birthplace of skiing, but Telemark is also a paradise for hikers in summer. Whether you're exploring on foot or by bike, the deserted lakes, thick forests and winding routes give you countless reasons to stay out in the open air.**

You can explore the Telemark region at leisure on board the two old steamers *Victoria* and *Henrik Ibsen (fare Skien–Dalen approx. 1,200 NOK, return half price, bike 200 NOK | tel. 40 92 00 00 | telemark-skanalen.no)* that depart from *Skien* on the south coast in the morning and drop anchor in *Dalen* in the heart of the Telemark in the early evening. If you have a bicycle, the return jour-ney along the banks of the Telemark Canal is a perfect finish to a holiday: You should plan two days for the 120km journey.

If you love nature, take a day trip through Telemark on a steamboat

SIGHTSEEING

RJUKAN

This village (pop. 3,300), which experienced a tremendous industrial boom at the turn of the 20th century, lies wedged between two massive mountain ranges. The day-long hike to *Gaustatoppen* (1,883m) table mountain is rewarded with a panoramic view over much of southern Norway. Rjukan became famous in 2013 when three huge sun mirrors were installed high above the town. Until their arrival, the town was overshadowed by the mountains from October to March. Now sunlight strikes the market square in winter, too. *visitrjukan.com*

SPORT & ACTIVITIES

BØ SOMMARLAND

Europe's largest water park. Children and adults alike can really let their hair down on the enormous water mountain and valley run, as well as a gigantic half pipe and artificial surfing wave. Particularly in the high summer season, it's easy to spend a whole day here. *Mid-June–mid-Aug daily 10am–6pm | admission 389 NOK, children (95–140cm) 359 NOK | Steintjønn-vegen 2 | Bø i Telemark | sommarland.no | ⊞ C17*

KRISTIANSAND

(⊞ B18) **Kristiansand is probably the only place in Norway that you'll get away with wearing a light summer dress and shorts.**

This harbour city (pop. 86,000) is regarded as the country's warmest spot and is a great place to relax, with white sandy beaches and optimal sailing conditions between the offshore islets. The range of activities for families, sun worshippers and water sports enthusiasts is second to none thanks to the beautiful skerry landscape on the Skagerrak strait. Unsurprisingly, the royals have a summer residence in Kristiansand. The right-angled grid layout of the streets was ordered by the Danish-Norwegian King Christian IV, who established the town on a sandy promontory in 1641.

SIGHTSEEING

SØRLANDETS KUNSTMUSEUM

The exhibitions in the contemporary-designed, light rooms present local art from the last 300 years. Some of the works portray the harsh lives of their painters in realistic detail. The coffee shop offers views of the surrounding area. *Thu–Sun 11am–5pm | admission 120 NOK; online tickets 110 NOK | Skippergata 24B | skmu.no | ⊙ 1 hr*

KRISTIANSAND MUSEUM

Open-air museum housing a total of 40 historic buildings. You can visit workshops and a small grocer's shop, as well as a miniature model town where you will suddenly feel like Gulliver. *Mid-June–mid-Aug daily 11am–4pm, otherwise shorter opening times | admission 110 NOK | Vigeveien 22B | vest agdermuseet.no | ⊙ 1 hr*

EATING & DRINKING

BAKGÅRDEN BAR & RESTAURANT

Locals love the inspiring and creative menu. Afterwards, head to the bar, which serves the town's finest cocktails and mocktails (without alcohol). *Tollbodgata 5A | tel. 38 02 12 11 | bakgardenbar.no | ££–£££*

SHOPPING

Kvadraturen, which refers to the right-angled grid layout of the town centre, is full of shops, cafés and restaurants. *Hansen & Co (Skippergata 14 | hansenco.no)* specialises in Scandinavian interior design, from functional to … just great! Take a break from shopping with a perfect latte macchiato at the tiny *Cuba Life* café *(Tollbodgata 6)*.

BEACHES

The small oases of sand between the boulders on the shore are popular places for swimming. There are also large sandy beaches at *Bertnes Bay* (3km east) and *Hamresanden* (11km east). These, along with *Bystranda* in Kristiansand and *Skotteviga* near Lillesand (31km east), are among the cleanest beaches in southern Norway.

AROUND KRISTIAN SAND

12 KAP LINDESNES

82km / 1½ hrs from Kristiansand (by car via E39)

This lighthouse on Norway's southern cape, built in 1915, stands on a small hill. The *Lighthouse Museum (summer daily 9am–8pm, rest of the year 10am–5pm | admission 80 NOK | lindesnesfyr.no)* was built by blasting

Enjoy the sunny side of Norway in Kristiansand

SIDER TIP
Under the lighthouse

away the rock and is well worth a visit. If you're travelling with a motorhome, you can sleep here for 100 NOK per night. Just 10km back towards Kristiansand, you'll find yourself in a secluded area at *Under (Bålyveien 48 | Lindesnes | under.no | booking at: exploretock. com/under | ££),* Norway's first half-sunken restaurant with spectacular Snøhetta architecture. The menu is created using ingredients that can be seen through the panoramic window. If you prefer to stay at sea level, make sure you at least take a look at the website. *B18*

13 MINERAL PARK

60km / 1 hr from Kristiansand (by car via Riksvei 9)

There is a lot more to see besides minerals and rocks at this park and children will have a great time digging and making things with the hands-on exhibits. The park also offers activities for the whole family to enjoy, including canoeing, sliding, climbing and more besides. *Late June–mid-Aug daily 10am–6pm | admission adults 259 NOK, children (3–13 years) 279 NOK | Mineralvegen 1 | Hornes | on Road 9 | mineralparken.no | ⏱ 2 hrs | B18*

14 RISØR ★

110km / 1½ hrs from Kristiansand (by car via E18)

This "white town on the Skaggerak" (pop. 6,900) has attractive wooden houses and impressive and elegant residences along the harbour promenade. It is the most important gathering place for lovers of wooden boats (festival beginning of August). The 19th-century Daymark *(Trappegata 5 | olasteen.no)* not only affords a great panoramic view over the town and the fjord, but also exhibits the artwork of local artist Ola Steen. *risor.no | C17–18*

THE WEST

IN THE HANDS OF THE RAIN GODS

What do you need to bring with you for a trip to the Norwegian fjords? Time – and preferably plenty of it. There's so much to see here: deep gorges, uninhabited coastline, endless stretches of land and powerful waterfalls all around you.

Speaking of water: the rain gods seem to be very much at home in western Norway and prove their power at any time of the day or year. Don't let this get the better of you! The phrase, "There's no such thing as bad weather, only bad clothing" seems to have been coined here.

Absolutely beautiful: Geirangerfjord with the Seven Sisters waterfall

When the sun does shine and the temperatures rise to a decent level, the archipelagos, fjords and mountains are bathed in white light. The museums, cafés and shops full of creative wares will have to wait for another day – now is the time to go out and enjoy nature on a hiking, rafting or fishing trip. And when the next rain falls, we'll see who the real Westerners are.

THE WEST

MARCO POLO HIGHLIGHTS

⭐ **PREIKESTOLEN**
A tiny rocky plateau soaring above the Lysefjord – an uplifting sight ➤ p.63

⭐ **HARDANGERVIDDA**
Europe's most extensive plateau area and the ultimate hiking experience at any time of the year ➤ p.65

⭐ **VØRINGFOSSEN**
Roaring waterfall in the heart of western Norway ➤ p.65

⭐ **BRYGGEN**
Stroll between the wooden houses in the old Hanseatic city of Bergen ➤ p.66

⭐ **BORGUND STAVKIRKE**
The jewel among Norway's stave churches ➤ p.71

⭐ **THE FLÅM RAILWAY**
A trip through steep mountain scenery ➤ p.72

⭐ **GEIRANGERFJORD**
Storybook western Norway ➤ p.75

⭐ **RUNDE**
Breeding colony for hundreds of thousands of birds ➤ p.76

Nordøyane

81km, 2 hrs

Godøy 8

Runde ⭐ 7

Ålesun
p.7

Sandøy

5 Vestkapp

Stadlandet

Sunnmøre

4 Nordfjord

Svanøy

E39

422km, 7¼ hrs

Sognefjord
p.71

Sula

221km, 3 hrs 20 mins

Sandøy

E16

One

Bryggen ⭐

Bergen
p.66

Hardang
p.

2 Troldhaugen
(Greig Museum & Home)

3 Lysøen

Huftarøy

Sunnhordland

E134

211km, 5¼ hrs

Bømlo

N o r s k e -
h a v e t

E39

282km, 5 hrs 20 mins

Karmøy

Boknafjorden

Stavanger
p.62

Preikestolen ⭐

1

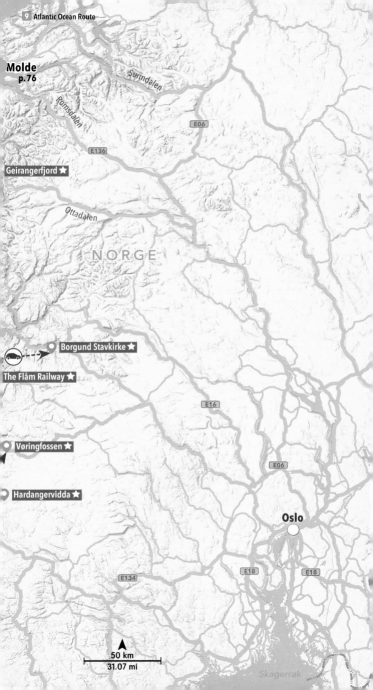

Molde
p.76

Sunndalen

Romsdalen

E06

E136

Geirangerfjord ★

Ottadalen

N O R G E

Borgund Stavkirke ★

The Flåm Railway ★

E16

Vøringfossen ★

E06

Hardangervidda ★

Oslo

E134

E18

E18

50 km
31.07 mi

Skagerrak

STAVANGER

(🏛 A17) **From a sleepy fishing village to a booming oil capital – Stavanger (pop. 145,000) shows how it's done.**

Life in the streets of the old town *(Gamle Stavanger),* to the west of Vågen harbour bay, is quite peaceful among the white wooden houses, while the shore on the other side is lined with shops, bars and restaurants. The "Colourful Street" is a real highlight, with each house painted in a different bright colour.

SIGHTSEEING

NORSK HERMETIKKMUSEUM
What could possibly be interesting about a museum for tinned food? Well, in this former canning factory you will feel as if the year is 1920 and at any minute you'll meet the workers who are canning the sardines and sending them out into the world. *Tue/Wed, Fri 11am–3pm, Thu 11am–7pm, Sat/Sun 11am–4pm | admission 100 NOK | Andasmauet 15 | iddismuseum.no | ⏱ 1 hr*

NORSK OLJEMUSEUM
The interactive oil museum shows how the use of the black gold has evolved, and how the offshore adventure has transformed Norway. *June–Aug daily 10am–7pm, Sept–May Mon–Sat 10am–4pm, Sun 10am–6pm | admission 150 NOK | Kjeringholmen 1 | norskolje.museum.no | ⏱ 1½ hrs*

EATING & DRINKING

BØKER OG BØRST
A cosy café and an insider tip among craft beer lovers: the menu includes over 200 varieties of beer (including local ones) *Øvre Holmegate 32 | tel. 51 86 04 76 | bokerogborst.no | ££*

SHOPPING

HANNES KERAMIKK
Here you'll find vases, cups and bowls in a simple Scandinavian style. They make great souvenirs for you to take home. *Øvre Strandgate 51A*

JANAS FISKERØKERI
Home of Norway's best smoked salmon, with some of the smoking ovens dating to the pre-war years. Gourmets from all over Europe regularly come to stock up on gravlax or smoked salmon. *Johannes gate 37*

INSIDER TIP
Famed smoked salmon

BEACHES

Thanks to the Ice Age and the Gulf Stream, there are wonderful sandy beaches with dunes for sunbathing near Stavanger. The Jæren beaches start to the south. The most delightful are *Borestranda* (around 15km south of the airport) and *Orrestranda* (22km to the south). The sandy *Sandvestranden*, which is surrounded by cliffs, is a little to the north of the picturesque harbour town Skudeneshavn in Karmøy (22km north of Stavanger, ferry). It offers a

If you aren't afraid of heights, climb Preikestolen for its wonderful views

magnificent view of the North Sea and plenty of room to stretch your legs even on warm summer days. If you haven't brought your swimming gear, hopefully you'll have packed a decent picnic.

NIGHTLIFE

It's really lively on the quay and in the small streets on the northern side of Vågen Bay. There's plenty of action until closing time *(clubs at 3.30am; other venues 2am)*. Cardinal Pub & Bar *(Skagen 21 | cardinal.no)* has Norway's largest selection of beer with more than 500 varieties.

AROUND STAVANGER

🄵 PREIKESTOLEN ★ 🚩

60km / 1 hr 20 mins from Stavanger (by car via E39 and Riksvei 13)

If you have managed the two-hour hike (one way) to the 604m-high plateau that only measures 625m² you'll be rewarded with the wonderful view over Lysefjord. There are no railings and no barriers to protect you here. While some still wrestle with their fear of heights, others sit down and boldly let their feet dangle into the abyss. Now is the time to set up the barbecue you've brought and have a picnic accompanied by the sublime scenery around you! *A-B17*

HARDANGER

(□ B15–16) **The Folgefonna glacier towers over the region of Hardanger beside the Hardangerfjord, which extends inland to the south of Bergen as far as the high Hardangervidda plateau.**

There are waterfalls in every direction: the *Steinsdalsfossen* in the west, the *Tveitefossen* in the north, the *Vøringfossen* in the east and the *Låtefossen* in the south. Especially when the snow melts, these watery wonders that are the "gate to Hardanger" spray their fine mist over all observers and their cars. If you don't mind getting a bit wet, you can walk along the routes behind the waterfall, such as at *Steinsdalsfossen*.

Hundreds of thousands of fruit trees grow between the forested slopes and the *Hardangerfjord*, which shimmers a bluish-green in summer. The blossoming fruit trees at the end of April – when people are still skiing just a few hundred metres further up the slope – are an absolute highlight.

SIGHTSEEING

HARDANGER FARTØYVERN SENTER (HARDANGER MUSEUM SHIPYARD)

Ever fancied building a real boat? Then try your luck here. Professionals will first show you how they repair old sailing boats and schooners and then it's your turn to swing the hammer. The shipyard exudes authentic charm with its smells of seawater, wood and tar.

Mountains and glaciers are within view at Hardangerfjord

Guided tours in summer and there's a café. *May–Aug daily 10am–5pm | admission 115 NOK | Norheimsund | fartoyvern.no | ⏱ 1½ hrs*

HARDANGERVIDDA ★

This is the largest high-altitude plateau in Europe, extending over an area of 9,000km², and is the Norwegian hiking area par excellence. The well-marked paths that criss-cross the barren, 1,000m- to 1,600m-high plateau only come to light between June and September. The flora is limited to stunted birch trees, grass and lichen but the fauna has many surprises in store: birds of prey, lemmings and Europe's most southerly reindeer herds.

The only real peaks are in the west; hiking is completely safe and nights can be spent in self-catering cabins or professionally run accommodation, or even in your own tent. The best places to start your hike on the "Vidda" are Road 7 on the northern border and the E134 on the southeastern periphery near *Røldal*. A strenuous but beautiful climb ends at *Munkentrappene* near *Lofthus* (Road 13) on the western border of the Hardangervidda, the route having been constructed by monks in the 13th century. An even more dramatic climb is from Kinsarvik through *Husedalen*, the "Valley of the Waterfalls".

NORSK NATURSENTER HARDANGER

Those who don't just want to hike across Hardangervidda can get a detailed overview of the natural and cultural history of the plateau at this centre. The kitchen staff in the restaurant *Hardangerviddahallen (tel. 53 67 40 00 | £)* conjure up excellent traditional meals. *April–14 June, 21 Aug–Oct daily noon–6pm, 15 June–20 Aug 10am–6pm | admission 160 NOK | Øvre Eidfjord | norsknatursenter.no | ⏱ 1 hr*

VØRINGFOSSEN ★

You'll hardly be able to see all the way down to the bottom of this easily accessible waterfall, but that makes the view over the thundering water and deep gorge all the more exciting. Please be careful and mind the guardrails! Twelve cubic metres of water plummet into the ravine every second. The gigantic *Sysendamm* is located just a few miles away towards the Hardangervidda. There you'll have a superb view of the valley and Hardangerjøkulen glacier.

EATING & DRINKING

STEINSTØ FRUKTGARD

This café serves fruit and berries from Hardanger, Norwegian home-style cooking, and a breathtaking view over the fjord and fjell. *Fykesundvegen 768 | Steinstø | on Road 7 | tel. 99 69 15 27 | steinsto.no | £*

VILTKROA

Organic gourmet meals at the campsite *Måbødalen Camping (Øvre Eidfjord | tel. 99 00 91 60 | mabodalen. no | ££)*: trout, reindeer and lots of veg.

BERGEN

(□ A15) **Yes, it's true: with 248 days of rain per year, Bergen has one of the highest rainfalls of any city on earth. Hardly a day goes by when there are no raindrops at all. But, when the sun does break through the clouds, cafés and restaurants quickly get full.**

Bergen was founded in 1070 and today has a population of 287,000, making it Norway's second-largest city. It has a glorious past as a royal seat, a port and a member of the Hanseatic League.

Bergen was the largest city in northern Europe in the Middle Ages. The Bryggen harbour quarter was in the hands of the Hansa from the 14th century and the last northern German merchants didn't leave until 1764.

The *Bergen Card (24 hrs 300 NOK | visitbergen.com)* offers a 15 per cent discount at the Bygarasjen

WHERE TO START?

Every route leads to **Torgallmenningen Square** and the **Fisketorget (fish market)** at the harbour. But first you should park in a car park or – coming from the south – near a *Bybanen* tram stop. You can then take the tram to the end station in the city centre. If you're arriving from the lake with a ferry or on a Hurtigruten ship, follow the signs to the nearest car park.

multistorey car park as well as free or substantially reduced entry fees to most of the sights in the city. If you plan to stay overnight in summer, you should book your accommodation well in advance.

SIGHTSEEING

BERGENSHUS FESTNING

The *Håkonshalle*, built in 1261 in the Gothic style, is the heart of the Bergenshus fortress complex (a landmark for sailors visible from afar) and is used today for concerts and other events. Construction of the neighbouring, massive *Rosary Tower* as a residence and defence installation was completed in 1568. *In summer daily 11am–5pm, otherwise shorter opening times | admission 120 NOK | bymuseet.no |* ⊙ *1 hr*

BRYGGEN ★

The colourful houses are worldfamous. Norway was in the hands of merchants from Lübeck for more than 400 years, which you can almost sense when you walk between houses and courtyards, even though many of the buildings were reconstructed after a major fire in 1702. The best place to start your walk is in the *Schøtstue*, where you'll see the merchants' meeting space and some exhibition pieces from the *Hanseatic Museum (museumvest.no)*, which is currently closed for renovation work. Then proceed to the historic *Finnegården* courtyard and past the shops with embroidery, pottery and artwork until you reach the *Bryggens Museum (May–Aug*

Superb with or without an umbrella: old merchants' houses in Bryggen

daily 11am–5pm, otherwise shorter opening times | admission 160 NOK | bymuseet.no). ⏱ *1 hr*

FLØYEN

This lookout hill has a firm place in the hearts of the people of Bergen; it rises up 319m above the town centre and provides a magnificent view over the city, surrounding islands and as far as the open sea. You can reach the summit in eight minutes with the *Fløiban (Mon–Fri 7.30am–11pm, Sat/Sun 8am–11pm | one-way fare 75 NOK | floibanen.no).* ⏱ *2 hrs*

FISKETORGET (FISH MARKET)

The prawns at the fish market are fresh and particularly tasty. They put them into three-cornered bags, allowing you to pull them out and eat them right there and then. If it's raining in Bergen, take shelter in the glass *Mathallen* on the southern shore or in the *Kjøttbasaren (kjøttbasaren.no)* and grab some food. ⏱ *1 hr*

AKVARIET 🏖 👫

You'll not only be able to see local marine animals in western Norway's largest aquarium; crocodiles, exotic ocean dwellers and snakes are also on display. Families with children will be delighted by the seals and penguins, and there is also a pool where you can put your hands in the water and actually touch the fish and crustaceans. *May–Aug daily 9am–6pm; otherwise 10am–6pm | admission 315 NOK, children (3–15 years) 200 NOK | akvariet.no |* ⏱ *2 hrs*

KODE

The acronym stands for the four collections of *Bergen's art museum*, which are situated almost bang next to each

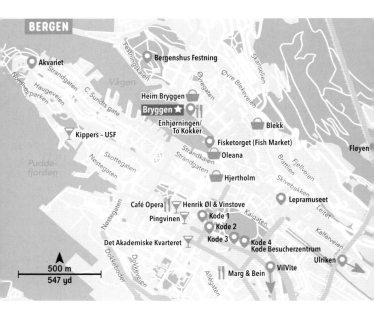

BERGEN

Akvariet
Strandgaten
Nordnes-parken
Haugeveien
C. Sundts gate
Vågen
Festningskaien
Bergenshus Festning
Øyregaten
Øvre Blekeveien
Skanseien
Heim Bryggen
Bryggen ★
Enhjørningen/
To Kokker
Blekk
Kippers – USF
Skottegaten
Nøstegaten
Fisketorget (Fish Market)
Strandkaien
Strandgaten
Oleana
Fløyen
Puddefjorden
Fjellveien
Batlien
Hjertholm
Skivebakken
Nøstegaten
Café Opera
Henrik Øl & Vinstove
Lepramuseet
Leitet
Pingvinen
Kode 1
Kaigaten
Kode 2
Det Akademiske Kvarteret
Kode 3
Kode 4
Kalfarveien
Dokkeboder
Dokkeveien
Kode Besucherzentrum
Ulriken
▲
500 m
547 yd
Allégaten
Marg & Bein
VilVite

other. *Kode 1 (Nordahl Bruns gate 1)* is dedicated to handicrafts and design; one of its special exhibits is the *Sölvskatten*, a collection of some 600 gold and silver items crafted in Bergen. *Kode 2 (Rasmus Meyer allé 6)* houses temporary international exhibits plus the café *Smakverket* on the ground floor – the perfect place for a break.

The famous Rasmus Meyer Collection featuring Norwegian works by artists such as Edvard Munch, Christian Krogh, JC Dahl, Harriet Backer and others graces the walls of *Kode 3 (Rasmus Meyer allé 7)*. It also has a noteworthy collection of sketches and graphics by Edvard Munch. The permanent exhibit in *Kode 4 (Rasmus Meyer allé 9)* takes you on a journey through art history from the Renaissance to the 20th

century. At the time of publishing this guide, Kode is closed for renovation work. The *Lysverket* art museum remains open. *May–Sept Tue/Wed, Fri–Sun 10am–5pm, Thu 10am–8pm, otherwise shorter opening times | admission 150 NOK, children accompanied by a paying adult go free | kodebergen.no | ⊙ 1 hr*

LEPRAMUSEET

Leprosy? A strange subject for a museum maybe, but a visit will provide a different perspective on this disease. Housed in the former Sankt Jørgens Hospital where Dr Armauer Hansen discovered the disease in 1873, the museum exhibits photos and historic documents recording the lives of

INSIDER TIP
Not for the faint-hearte

leprosy patients and their fates. Be warned: some of the photos are rather gruesome to look at. *In summer Mon–Thu 11am–6pm, Fri–Sun 11am–3pm | admission 120 NOK | Kong Oscars gate 59 | bymuseet.no | ⏱ 1 hr*

ULRIKEN

On the cable car ride to the highest peak in Bergen, the view of the city and its surrounding area expands with every metre that you climb. Bergen's mountain basin location, the countless offshore islands and even ships on the horizon come into view if the weather conditions are favourable. Once you've reached the top, you should take the time for a hike through the alpine landscape on Ulriken's ridge. *Cable car May–Sept daily 9am–11pm; Oct–April Tue/Wed, Sun 9am–7pm, Thu–Sat 9am–11pm | return trip 195 NOK | Ulriken Express bus May–Sept daily 9am–6.30pm every 30 mins from the centre (Torgallmenningen 1A), return 100 NOK*

VILVITE 🐵

In this science centre, children and young people in particular will be able to immerse themselves in the world of natural science and technology. Among the many subjects dealt with are weather, energy and the ocean. With experiments, an underwater world, ship and oil rig simulators, a café and a shop. *Thu–Fri 9am–3pm, Sat/Sun 10am–5pm | admission 195 NOK, children (3–15 years) 165 NOK | Thormøhlens gate 51 | vilvite.no | ⏱ 2 hrs*

EATING & DRINKING

CAFÉ OPERA

This small café-restaurant has been popular for almost 30 years, largely because of its location between the university and city centre as well as its short menu of excellent dishes and its dedication to providing a stage for music and art. *Engen 18 | cafeopera.org | £*

ENHJØRNINGEN/TO KOKKER

Bergen's best fish dishes are served in *Enhjørningen (tel. 55 30 69 50 | enhjorningen.no)* in the Hanseatic Enhjørningsgården courtyard in Bryggen. To Kokker (tel. 55 30 69 55 | tokokker.no) in the same building specialises in hearty meat dishes. *Enhjørningsgården 29 | £££*

MARG & BEIN

Not far from the university, the award-winning chef Hanne Frosta offers fans of refined cuisine just what they are looking for. How about pollack and seaweed or herring and trout roe? All the ingredients are sourced fresh from the sea and from the region. *Fosswinckelsgate 18 | tel. 55 32 34 32 | marg-bein.no | ££*

INSIDER TIP
Fresh from the sea

SHOPPING

BLEKK

This small art shop can be found in the lane to the right, underneath Fløibanen train station. It sells countless prints and original works by Norwegian artists. *Lille Øvregate 12*

HEIM BRYGGEN

Among all the design and kitchen pieces, you're sure to find something nice to take home here, whether it's stylish or useful. Everything is made in Norway. *Bredsgården 1B*

HJERTHOLM

This shop, on the fifth floor in the *Galleriet* shopping arcade in the middle of Bergen's main shopping street, sells all types of artwork. If you can't find anything you like here, there are around 60 other shops to browse. *Torgallmenningen 8*

OLEANA

Opposite Bryggen, at the harbour, there's a small, cute, and colourful shop selling excellent knitted clothes. The swirling patterns of roses, leaves and vines on the knitwear are inspired by the decorations on old fishing boats. *Strandkaien 2A | oleana.no*

INSIDER TIP Perfectly knitted

NIGHTLIFE

DET AKADEMISKE KVARTERET

For students by students: if you're looking for somewhere to make friends, this is the place. You're sure to get good information and have nice conversations. *Olav Kyrres gate 49 | kvarteret.no*

HENRIK ØL & VINSTOVE

This is also a great place to start your evening. An extensive selection of British, German and Norwegian beers, not too much noise and friendly people in front of – and behind – the bar. *Engen 10*

KIPPERS – USF

On warm summer evenings, take a stroll around the city soaking in its beguiling vibes. Start your evening at this coffee shop. With a bit of luck, the other guests will point you in the direction of the coolest place to head to next. *Georgernes verft 12 | usf.no*

PINGVINEN

Totally trendy, with a relaxed atmosphere, an extensive list of beers and traditional Norwegian food *(€)*. *Vaskerelven 14 | tel. 55 60 46 46*

Edvard Grieg and his wife Nina lived at Troldhaugen House

AROUND BERGEN

2 TROLDHAUGEN (GRIEG MUSEUM & HOME)

10km / 15 mins from Bergen/centre (Bybanen tram from the "Hop" stop)
For 22 years, between spring and autumn, this villa on a promontory in Nordåsvannet Lake was the home of Edvard Grieg and his wife Nina. The small cabin near the water that Grieg used for composing inspired him to write many famous works. Concerts are held regularly in summer in the hidden-away Troldsalen, including the 30-minute lunchtime concerts with a tour of the house and museum *(Tue–Sun 11.30am and 1pm | 200 NOK). May–Sept Tue–Sun 10am–5pm | admission 130 NOK | Troldhaugveien 65 | grieg museum.no | ⊙ 2 hrs | ⊞ A15*

> **INSIDER TIP**
> **Classic time out**

3 LYSØEN

25km / 40 mins from Bergen (by car via E39)
The country home of Bergen's virtuoso violinist Ole Bull (1810–88) on a small island in Fanafjord is built in a rustic mix of styles and is well worth seeing. The *museum (⊙ 1 hr)* was undergoing renovation work at the time of publishing this guide. The island itself is worth visiting too: make the trip in style with the boat from *Buena kai (May–Sept Tue–Sun 11am–3pm every hr. | 50 NOK return) lysoen.no | ⊞ A16*

SOGNEFJORD

(⊞ A–B14–15) **A gigantic estuary and towering mountains on both sides characterise Norway's longest and deepest fjord.**

Even today, travellers have to rely on the ferries that cross the fjord throughout the day. Some of the side arms of the Sognefjord are famous natural tourist attractions. The Aurlandsfjord and Nærøyfjord – one of the narrowest navigable fjords – are UNESCO World Heritage Sites.

SIGHTSEEING

BALESTRAND

The countryside and the light have attracted artists to this small village at the widest point of Sognefjord for 150 years. Peace and quiet reign among the pretty houses – which include some galleries – and the view over the fjord is unsurpassed. You can drop into the *Kviknes Hotel (kviknes.no)*, a Swiss-style fairytale hotel, and try a prawn sandwich at the *Balholm Bar & Bistro*. The ferry from Balestrand to Fjærland *(June–mid-Sept daily 8am and noon | return 540 NOK)* steers north-wards through Fjærlandfjord directly towards an arm of *Jostedalsbreen*, the largest glacier in continental Europe.

> **INSIDER TIP**
> **A pleasant crossing**

BORGUND STAVKIRKE ★ ⚑

The most famous of Norway's stave churches (built around 1180) is on the E16, 30km to the east of Lærdal, a small town at the eastern end of Sognefjord. The dragon heads on the gable and wonderful carvings on the western entrance are especially striking. If there are too many tourists, it might be worth changing your plans and visiting the small *Undredal stave church. Mid-April–mid-Oct daily 9.30am–5.30pm | admission 100 NOK | stavkirke.no | ⓒ 1 hr*

THE FLÅM RAILWAY ★
Past gushing waterfalls, deep ravines and through narrow tunnels – without exaggeration, this is the world's most spectacular train ride. The train runs from *Myrdal* at a height of 866m down the mountain to the small town of *Flåm*, the journey taking approximately one hour. If you prefer to stretch your legs and take in the spectacular scenery at a slower pace, you take the train up the mountain to Myrdal instead and then ride back down the valley by bike. *Fares from 650 NOK | visitflam.com*

NORSK BREMUSEUM
This architecturally interesting museum focuses on Jostedalsbreen glacier and includes exhibitions, models and a wide-screen film. It is located in Fjærland at the foot of the Bøyabreen and Suphellebreen glacier arms. *April/May and Sept/Oct daily 10am–4pm; June–Aug 9am–7pm | admission 140 NOK | bre.museum.no | ⓒ 1½ hrs*

UNDREDAL STAVKIRKE
The smallest church in Scandinavia lies hidden between the towering mountain scenery on the shore of Aurlandsfjord, 13km to the north of Flåm. The church is only 4m wide and was probably built in the 12th century. The village of Undredal is also famous for its goat's cheese. ⓒ *30 mins*

STEGASTEINEN 🐾
While paragliders use the platform as a jumping-off point, everyone else stands behind the railing to admire the spectacular view of the fjord (if good weather prevails). You have two options to return to safe ground – paraglide or simply walk down the 30m – which will you go for? *On the Aurlandsvegen pass road between Aurland and Lærdal, turn off shortly after Aurland*

AROUND SOGNEFJORD

▣ NORDFJORD
169km / 3 hrs from Balestrand to Olden (by car and ferry via Fylkesvei 55 and Riksvei 5)
Pretty villages and high hills that invite tourists to take long hikes lie on both sides of Nordfjord beneath the gigantic *Jostedalsbreen glacier*. Trips to the *Briksdalsbreen glacier snout (May–Oct daily 9am–5pm | pre-book at tel. 57 87 68 05 | 250 NOK | briksdal. no)* start in *Oldedalen*, 22km after the signposted turn-off in *Olden*. A more economical alternative is to travel along the Loenvatnet Lake from *Loen* to the valley end at *Kjenndal*. From

Borgund Stave Church: timber construction from the 12th century

there, it is only a 15-minute walk to the arm of the *Kjenndalsbreen glacier*.

The *Loen Skylift (tickets from 555 NOK/return | loenskylift.no)* in Loen is spectacular at all times of the year, leading up the 1,011m-high mountain *Hoven*. Keep calm while you travel up the steepest ski lift in the world! You'll reach the top in just seven minutes and will have a fantastic view over the fjord landscape. Then, clip on your skis and off you go! Or put your rucksack on your back and tackle the descent on foot. Remember: the lift can also take you down again. ⟦ *B14*

INSIDER TIP *Reach for the sky*

5 VESTKAPP

230km / 4 hrs 15 mins from Balestrand to Selje (by car and ferry via Riksvei 5 and E39)

Ships depart for the ruins of the *Selje Monastery (mid-June–mid-Aug daily 10.15am–1.15pm several departures | guided tour 399 NOK | tickets from the Tourist Information Office | tel. 40 44 60 11 | fjordguidingselje.no)* from the harbour at *Selje*. The monastery was erected in the 12th century in honour of St Sunniva, the patron saint of western Norway. You'll discover a wonderful sandy beach in *Ervik*, below Vestkapp. The almost 500m-high rock *Kjerringa* towers over the Stadlandet coast that is feared for its changing winds and currents. ⟦ *A–B13–14*

Stop for a bite at the port: you're always near the water in Ålesund

ÅLESUND

(*B13*) **The port city of Ålesund (pop. 67,000) is surrounded by numerous islands and has a delightful Art Nouveau charm. It's also the starting point for trips to the Geirangerfjord.**

German Emperor Wilhelm II had a weakness for this area and supported reconstruction efforts after the big fire here in 1904 when, in a single day, 850 houses were burnt to the ground, making 10,000 people homeless. The buildings were replaced in the subsequent years by magnificent, adorned houses and a tranquil fishing town became a jewel that's still impressive today.

SIGHTSEEING

JUGENDSTILSENTERET

An exhibition in the former Swan Chemists gives an impression of the architectural style that characterises Ålesund. The authentic furnishings make visitors feel they're back at the beginning of the 20th century. *June–Aug daily 10am–4pm | admission 110 NOK | Apotekergata 16 | vitimusea.no |* ☺ *2 hrs*

AKSLA

The hill above Ålesund is not to be missed. You can either climb the 418 steps to the top or follow the signs to *Fjellstua* in your car. The view sweeps over the town and its harbour, the neighbouring islands, straits and the sea. And, to the south, the snow-capped peaks of the Sunnmøre Alps come into view: it's sheer magic!

SUNNMØRE MUSEUM

Fifty-five old houses and thirty old boats, including Viking ships and a copy of a trading ship from the 11th century, can be seen in this open-air museum. *June-Aug Mon-Fri 10am-4pm, Sat/Sun noon-4pm, otherwise shorter opening times | admission 110 NOK | Museumsvegen 12 | approx. 5km east of the inner city | vitimusea. no | ⊙ 1 hr*

ATLANTIC SEA PARK 🐳

Several landscaped tanks have been carefully imbedded in the maritime environment of Norway's most modern aquarium. The largest pool contains four million litres of water and is home to all of the species of fish that live off the coast of western Norway. The daily highlight is when a diver heads underwater to feed the fish. You can find out much more about the sea and marine research in the science centre. *June-Aug daily 9am-5pm, otherwise Mon-Sat 11am-4pm, Sun until 6pm | admission: adults 225 NOK, children 100 NOK | Tueneset | atlanterhavsparken.no | ⊙ 1½ hrs*

EATING & DRINKING

ANNO

A few surprises are hidden in the menu of this Italian pizza place, including a pizza with dried cod which you probably can't get anywhere else. The focaccia with seafood delicacies is a treat for your taste buds and perfect in this maritime setting. *Apotekergata 9 | tel. 71 70 70 77 | anno.no | ££*

SHOPPING

DEVOLDFABRIKKEN ☂

The factory on the other side of the fjord not only sells the Devold pullovers that are so popular with seafarers, it has extended its range to include sport and leisure clothing made by other manufacturers. Plus there's a café and a magnificent view of the islands off Ålesund. *Mon-Fri 10am-8pm, Sat until 6pm, July/Aug also Sun noon-5pm | passenger ferry to Langevåg from the quay at the central buś station (return Mon-Fri 82 NOK, Sun 60 NOK) | devoldfabrikken.no*

SPORT & ACTIVITIES

KAYAK TOURS

The Storfjord, the "Great Fjord", stretches inland from Ålesund. This is the perfect route for day-long excursions into the fjord world. If you didn't bring your kayak with you and would like to join a group, outdoor trips are organised by companies such as *Actin* (tel. 92 09 57 45 | actin.no).

AROUND ÅLESUND

🖸 GEIRANGERFJORD ★

110km / 2½ hrs from Ålesund (by car and ferry via E136 and Fylkesvei 63)
The most famous destination and photo opportunity in western Norway: Geirangerfjord forces its way inland, surrounded by steep walls of rock,

magnificent waterfalls and mountain massifs with hidden alpine farms.

You can reach the village of *Geiranger* by water from *Hellesylt* (80km south-east of Ålesund on Road 60) with the *car ferry (8 departures daily | fare 335 NOK, car and driver 670 NOK)* or via winding roads. If you take *Road 63* from the south, the view from Dalsnibba (1,450m, toll) will give you the first impression of what awaits visitors to Geirangerfjord. From Åndalsnes *(ɰ B13),* the *Trollstigveien* hairpin bends with their spectacular lookout points, and the observation point of *Ørnesvingen* offer magnificent vistas of the Sunnmøre Alps. *ɰ B14*

⁊ RUNDE ★
120km / 2 ½ hrs from Ålesund (by car and ferry via E 39)

To the west of the island in the Ålesund shipping channel is a densely populated bird rock whose the most important attraction is the hundreds of thousands of colourful puffins that spend the summer here. The hike up to the cliffs takes about one hour and you'll not only be rewarded by the birds but also the magnificent view over the Norwegian Sea and the bracing ocean wind. Boat trips to the bird island depart from Ålesund. *ɰ A13*

⒏ GODØY
21km / 30 mins from Ålesund (by car via Fylkesvei 658)

Two underwater tunnels and a bridge lead to this small island off the coast of Ålesund. On the way, you can visit the island of *Giske* with its beautifully located marble church from the 11th century. The *Alnys fyr* lighthouse *(Tue–Sun 11am–5pm | tours 70 NOK)* that was erected on Godøy in 1936 is an important land-mark. A café serves delicious home-made cakes and snacks. Be sure to stay until the sun dips below the horizon. The panoramic view is sensational. *ɰ B13*

INSIDER TIP
Sensationa
sunset

MOLDE

(ɰ B13) **This quiet backwater (pop. 32,000) is turned on its head every year when internationally famous jazz musicians arrive here to jam at its annual festival.**

The surrounding countryside has a lot to offer with its exciting juxtaposition of mountains, fjords and the open sea. There's a splendid view of the Romsdalen peaks from the small Varden Mountain (407m) on the northern outskirts of the town.

SIGHTSEEING

KRONA ROMSDALSMUSEET
The museum building seems to stand like a lofty ship's mast in its surroundings. For art lovers, there's a permanent exhibition dedicated to the German painter Kurt Schwitters, who lived on the island of Hjertøya from 1932 to 1939. *June–Aug daily 11am–5pm, otherwise shorter opening times | admission 100 NOK | Per Amdams veg 4 | romsdalsmuseet.no | ◷ 1½ hrs*

AROUND MOLDE

EATING & DRINKING

FOLE GODT

Urban café culture at a latitude of 62 degrees: this cosy, authentic coffee shop tempts you to take a well-earned break. Everything is home-baked and made with love. The sandwiches are delicious – try the one filled with roast beef and *rémoulade* made according to their own recipe. *Storgata 61*

SPORT & ACTIVITIES

CYCLING ALONG THE SEA

Get in the saddle and discover the islands around Molde from your bike. When hopping around the islands, you'll hardly see any cars and can enjoy the taste of salt on your lips and the view of still bays nearby. The trip from Molde around the three islands is around 200km.

⑨ ATLANTIC OCEAN ROUTE 🐷

46km / 45 mins from Molde to Bud (by car via Fylkesvei 64)

This route starts in the idyllic fishing village of Bud and proceeds northwards along the Hustadvika section of the coast that was feared by seafarers on account of its unpredictable winds and currents – and you can be assured that you will still have close contact with the elements! You travel over eight bridges that connect small islands and skerries to the island of Averøya and further to the port of Kristiansund (*visitkristiansund.com*). There are places to stop and even go fishing on both sides of the road. 📖 *B12–13*

There's space on the smallest rock: puffins on the bird island of Runde

TRØNDELAG

IN THE FOOTSTEPS OF THE VIKING KINGS

The final resting place of Saint Olav, Nidaros Cathedral in Trondheim, was the most important place of pilgrimage in the north for 400 years. Today, it's the centre of Norwegian cultural history, reached easily on foot, by plane or by car.

If you want to submerge yourself in the area for a while, you'll find the peace and quiet you seek on the St Olav Way from Oslo to Trondheim *(pilegrimsleden.no)*. Around 170km of the route runs through the rugged expanses of Trøndelag, one of the few areas in

The red "Gate to Happiness": the old city bridge in Trondheim

Europe where, with a bit of luck, you can walk for days across fertile plains and past rivers full of salmon without seeing another soul; but you will see lots of sheep, reindeer and moose. The route is well signposted so you can rely on your all-weather jacket, tent and camping stove rather than on your GPS. You can boost your supplies with fish from the river and blueberries from the shrubs. This is all you will need for a bit of quiet, serenity and a little adventure.

TRØNDELAG

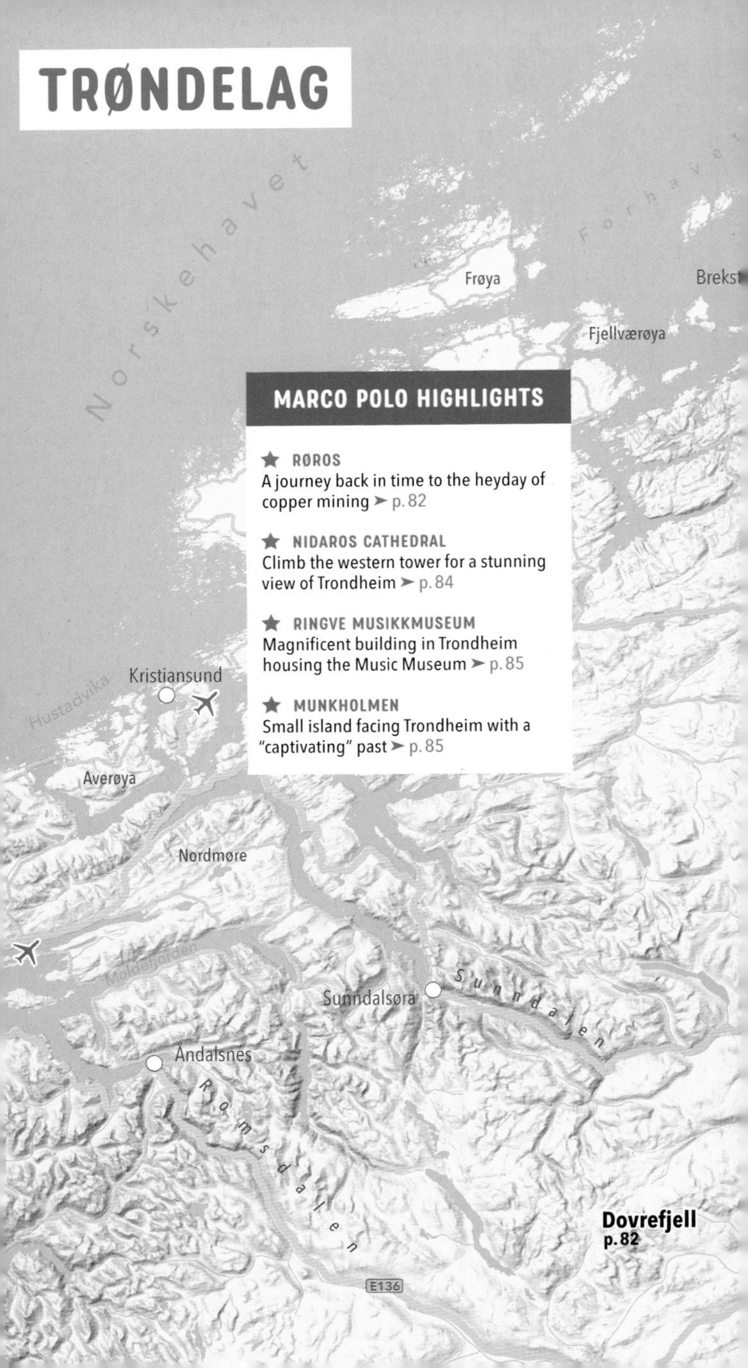

Norskehavet

Forhavet

Frøya

Breks

Fjellværøya

MARCO POLO HIGHLIGHTS

★ **RØROS**
A journey back in time to the heyday of copper mining ➤ p. 82

★ **NIDAROS CATHEDRAL**
Climb the western tower for a stunning view of Trondheim ➤ p. 84

★ **RINGVE MUSIKKMUSEUM**
Magnificent building in Trondheim housing the Music Museum ➤ p. 85

★ **MUNKHOLMEN**
Small island facing Trondheim with a "captivating" past ➤ p. 85

Kristiansund

Hustadvika

Averøya

Nordmøre

Moldefjorden

Sunndalsøra

Sunndalen

Åndalsnes

Romsdalen

Dovrefjell
p. 82

E136

Steinkjer

F o s n a

Beitstadfjorden

1 Den Gyldne Omvei

Verdalsøra

Ytterøy

Levanger

E06

Ringve Musikkmuseum ★

Trondheims-
fjorden

Stjørdal

E14

Munkholmen ★

Trondheim
p.84

Nidaros Cathedral ★

Orkanger   E39

154km, 2¼ hrs

G a u d a l e n

NORGE

pdal

Røros ★
p. 82

Tynset

25 km
15.54 mi

DOVREFJELL

(📖 C13–14) **Dovrefjell mountain region is the gateway to Trøndelag.**

Don't forget your binoculars and camera for your tour through the *Dovrefjell-Sunndalsfjella National Park*, so that you can take in the area's magnificent wildlife. The 300 musk oxen are the highlight of the mountainous region with the 2,286m-high *Snøhetta* peak. They're one of very few herds left in the world and you can only see them close up on a guided *safari (from Kongsvold or Oppdal | mid-June–Oct from 10am | duration approx. 7 hrs | 550 NOK | moskus safari.no)*. If you want to travel through the national park without a guide, make sure you take plenty of breaks. Websites like *nasjonalparkriket.no* provide more information. You will be rewarded with a fascinating view of the animals of this region, such as reindeer, wolverine, foxes, moose and mountain hawks. The *Oppdal Skisenter (oppdalskisenter.no)* is popular with mountaineers in winter.

SIGHTSEEING

The *Kongsvold Fjeldstue hotel (frich. no/kongsvold-fjeldstue)* has a long history as a mountain guesthouse and is, at the same time, also a botanical and zoological research station. A fantastic place to enjoy the mountains of the Dovrefjell-Sunndalsfjella National Park is the Snøhetta viewpoint – a

INSIDER TIP
Stylish lookout

beautiful, prize-winning construction made of glass, wood and steel situated at a height of 1,500m. If you leave from Hjerkinn, drive west to the Tverrfjellet car park and then the last 1.5km is an easy walk.

RØROS

(📖 D13) **Time seems to have come to a standstill in the former copper-mining town of ★ Røros (pop. 5,600), near the Swedish border.**

The church – the only stone building as far as the eye can see – towers above the rows of around 50 listed wooden houses on the two main streets. Røros is a winter-holiday resort: the temperature can sink to minus 30°C. The 🛷 sledding slopes at *Hummelfjell* are incredible and will definitely get a write-up in children's diaries as "the best experience ever".

SIGHTSEEING

SMELTHYTTA (SMELTERY) & OLAVSGRUVA (OLAV'S PIT)

Copper ore defined life in this region for 333 years. The work there was very hard, but there was always enough to eat. The smelting works provide an impressive insight into the tough life of the miners. If you want to delve deeper (literally) into history, you can descend into Olav's Pit. *Smelthytta June–Aug daily 10am–6pm, otherwise shorter opening times | admission 130 NOK |*

INSIDER TIP
Underground history

Olavsgruva (approx. 13km east on Road 31) | tours 20 June–15 Aug daily 9am, 11am, 1pm and 3pm, 16 Aug–10 Sept daily 3pm | admission 180 NOK | rorosmuseet.no | ⏱ 1¼ hrs each with tour

EATING & DRINKING

KAFFESTUGGU

While the atmosphere seems to have remained unchanged since the 18th century, the short but refined menu is very much of the present. In summer, the cosy rear courtyard provides the perfect spot for a cinnamon cappuccino in the open air. *Bergmannsgate 18 | tel. 72 41 10 33 | kaffestuggu.no | ££*

LOCAL FOOD SAFARI

INSIDER TIP
Gastronomic tour

The five-hour bus trip includes tastings of reindeer, elk, venison and trout plus a visit to a game slaughterhouse and a farm bakery, as well as lunch in a historic inn. *Daily in summer 11am–12.30pm | 625 NOK | book by the day before at 5.30pm at Røros Turistkontor (Peder Hiorts gate 2 | tel. 72 41 00 00 | roros.no)*

SHOPPING

Treat yourself to something nice after visiting the area: at *Røros Tweed (Tollef Bredalsvei 8 | rorostweed.no)*, you will find beautiful woven woollen throws in gorgeous colours that would look great on any bed or sofa. The accessories aren't exactly cheap, but you're bound to find a bargain or two at the factory outlet.

Shopping in the old copper city: the centre of Røros

TRONDHEIM

(□ D12) **Trondheim was the capital of Norway from 1030 to 1217, and the seat of the Norwegian archbishops until the Reformation in the 16th century. Pilgrims also made the trek to the town as they believed that Saint Olav's tomb was buried beneath the cathedral.**

The *Nidarosdomen (Nidaros Cathedral)* is Norway's only cathedral and the most important sight in the city (pop. 210,000), best known today for its University of Technology and internationally renowned research institutions.

SIGHTSEEING

STIFTSGÅRDEN

The 58m-long courtyard was completed in 1778 and the rooms and furnishings are in the Rococo style. When today's Kind Harald was young,

WHERE TO START?

Nidaros Cathedral: This is both your first stop and your starting point. You can reach it by car via the E6. Coming from the south, turn off into the Lade suburb and park at the *City Syd Shopping Centre*, which has a regular bus service to the centre. From the north, follow signs to the centre and the *Leuthenhaven multi-storey car park (closed Sun | Erling Skakkes gate 40).*

he used to run around on the wooden floors here. *June–20 Aug Mon-Sat 10am–3pm, Sun noon–3pm, tours every hr | admission 120 NOK | Munkegata 23 | ☉ 1 hr*

GAMLE BYBRO (OLD CITY BRIDGE)

Are you superstitious? If you are, there's nothing like walking through the "Gate to Happiness", as the Trondheimers lovingly call this bridge. It was built in 1861 and leads from the city centre to the *Bakklandet* district with its narrow streets and pretty wooden houses.

NIDAROS CATHEDRAL ★

Where can you find Bob Dylan? Walk up the stairs to the top of the west tower and you'll see a statue of the Archangel Michael which has an uncanny likeness to the singer and Nobel Prize winner. Enjoy the views over the town before descending into Scandinavia's largest medieval building, which has welcomed many a royal guest, the last being Princess Märtha Louise who married Ari Behn here in 2002. *June–Aug Mon–Fri 9am–6pm, Sat 9am–1pm, Sun 1–5pm, otherwise shorter opening times | admission 120 NOK | nidarosdomen.no | ☉ 1½ hrs*

ERKEBISPEGÅRDEN

The basement of the archbishop's palace houses the insignia of the Norwegian monarchy. To date, the crown and sceptre have been brought out of the glass cabinet for four coronations and two consecrations. Take a look before Crown Prince Haakon wears them next at his coronation in the nearby Nidaros Cathedral. *June–Aug Mon–Fri 10am–5pm, Sat 11am–3pm, Sun noon–4pm | admission 120 NOK or 240 NOK (including the cathedral, archbishop's courtyard and royal insignia) |* ⏱ *1 hr*

NORDENFJELDSKE KUNSTINDUSTRIMUSEUM

If you have a soft spot for design and furnishings, you absolutely must visit this museum, containing 400 years of Norwegian interior design, as well as Japanese works of art and unique Art Nouveau pieces. The range of works is broad, making the exhibition exciting and versatile. Because of renovation work, parts of the exhibition are currently in the *Hannah Ryggen Centre (Mon–Thu 9am–7pm, Fri 9am–3.30pm, Sat 11am–3pm | admission free | arrival by high-speed boat)* in Brekstad. *Munkegata 3-7 | nkim.no |* ⏱ *1 hr*

ROCKHEIM

Would you be a good professional musician? Give it a go and find your creative spark here: compose hip-hop loops on professional equipment, try out being a DJ or spray the walls with graffiti. This "time tunnel" documenting Norwegian rock and pop music will give you a few A-ha moments! *Tue–Sun 11am–6pm | admission 140 NOK | Brattøykaia 14 | rockheim.no |* ⏱ *1 ½ hrs*

RINGVE MUSIKKMUSEUM ★ 👥

Eighteenth-century *Ringve Gård* manor house is situated in a magnificent park on the eastern outskirts of

A millennium of history at Nidaros Cathedral in Trondheim

the city and is now the site of a music history museum. It is even possible to play some of the 2,000 instruments (at *prøv selv-stasjoner* – try-it-yourself stations) that are exhibited in a renovated barn. *June–Aug daily 10am–5pm, Sept–May Tue–Sun 11am–4pm | admission 160 NOK, children and young people up to 15 years free | Lade | ringve.no |* ⏱ *2 hrs*

MUNKHOLMEN ★

The small island in the fjord facing the city is home to some very well-preserved monastic ruins. This is where chiefs were beheaded in Viking days. The monastery was erected at the beginning of the 11th century and,

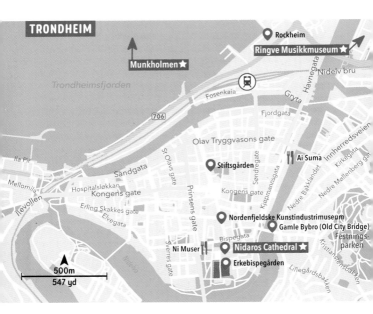

from 1658, was used as a fortress and prison. There are delightful views of the city and fjord from bathing places on the island. *Ferry every hr from 10am–5pm in summer | return fare 110 NOK | from Ravnkloa dock by the fish hall*

The delights from the café's own pastry shop are particularly

INSIDER TIP
Sweet heaven

popular, so leave space for some tasty cheesecake with fresh raspberries. *Bispegata 9a | tel. 73 53 63 11 | nimuser.no | ££*

EATING & DRINKING

AI SUMA
Italian cooking meets upscale Norwegian ingredients in an old granary situated on the prettiest stretch of the River Nidelv. *Kjøpmannsgate 57 | tel. 73 54 92 71 | aisuma.no | £££*

NI MUSER
This trendy café offers a selection of light refreshments, such as salads and sandwiches, depending on the season.

SHOPPING

You'll find all sorts of places here. First get your shoes shined at *C. V. Vingsand – Shoeshine (Olav Tryggvasons gate 8)* and then head to the interiors shop *Ting (Olav Tryggvasons gate 10)*, or to *Papir & Design (Thomas Angellsgate 22)*, where you'll discover stylish accessories made of paper and creative ideas to take home with you.

SPORT & ACTIVITIES

Trampe CycloCable, the only bicycle lift in the world, is Trondheim's secret attraction. It takes only 60 seconds to get you to the top of the 130m-long Brubakken road. All you need is a key-card, which you can get for free at the *Turistinformasjon (visittrondheim.no)*, and a bike. Then, off you go!

NIGHTLIFE

Trondheim attracts a young and relaxed crowd. Start your evening at *Antikvariatet (Nedre Bakklandet 4)* with a beer and a good book. Be sure to stay for the jazz concert later on in the evening. And don't forget to "Kiss the Prince" – if Crown Prince Haakon isn't there, then at least try a cocktail with the same name, served at the *Raus Bar (Nordre gate 21)*.

AROUND TRONDHEIM

■ DEN GYLDNE OMVEI
100km / almost 2 hrs by train to Røra
The "Golden Detour" branches off from the E6 north of Verdal and follows Roads 755 and 761 across the peninsula of *Inderøya*, passing galleries, bakeries and farm shops. If the weather cooperates, go for a cycling tour or head to Trondheimsfjord for some fishing. *visitinnherred.com* | *⠀D11–12*

Historic timber houses: a perfect backdrop for enjoying the moment

THE NORTH

BEYOND THE ARCTIC CIRCLE

The fascinating land of midnight sun and polar nights begins where the land peters into a narrow stretch, with the Norwegian coast just 6km from the Swedish border at its narrowest.

More extreme conditions can be expected here. Inhabitants of this sparsely populated area have got used to the unpredictable seasons and weather. Their lives are shaped by the Norwegian Sea – many work as fishers, seafarers or, more recently, on upstream oil rigs. In this area, far from where the king reigns in the city, the tone is coarser,

The strongest tidal current in Norway: Saltstraumen in Bodø

the dialect more pronounced, the jokes raunchier, but the people are genuine and welcoming.

Only two routes make their way northwards: one is the E6, a scenic route that leads through the Arctic Circle at Mo i Rana with a latitude of 66 degrees. The other involves going by boat through Arctic nature and having your breath taken away by the frayed chain of islands on the coast from aboard a Hurtigruten ship.

THE NORTH

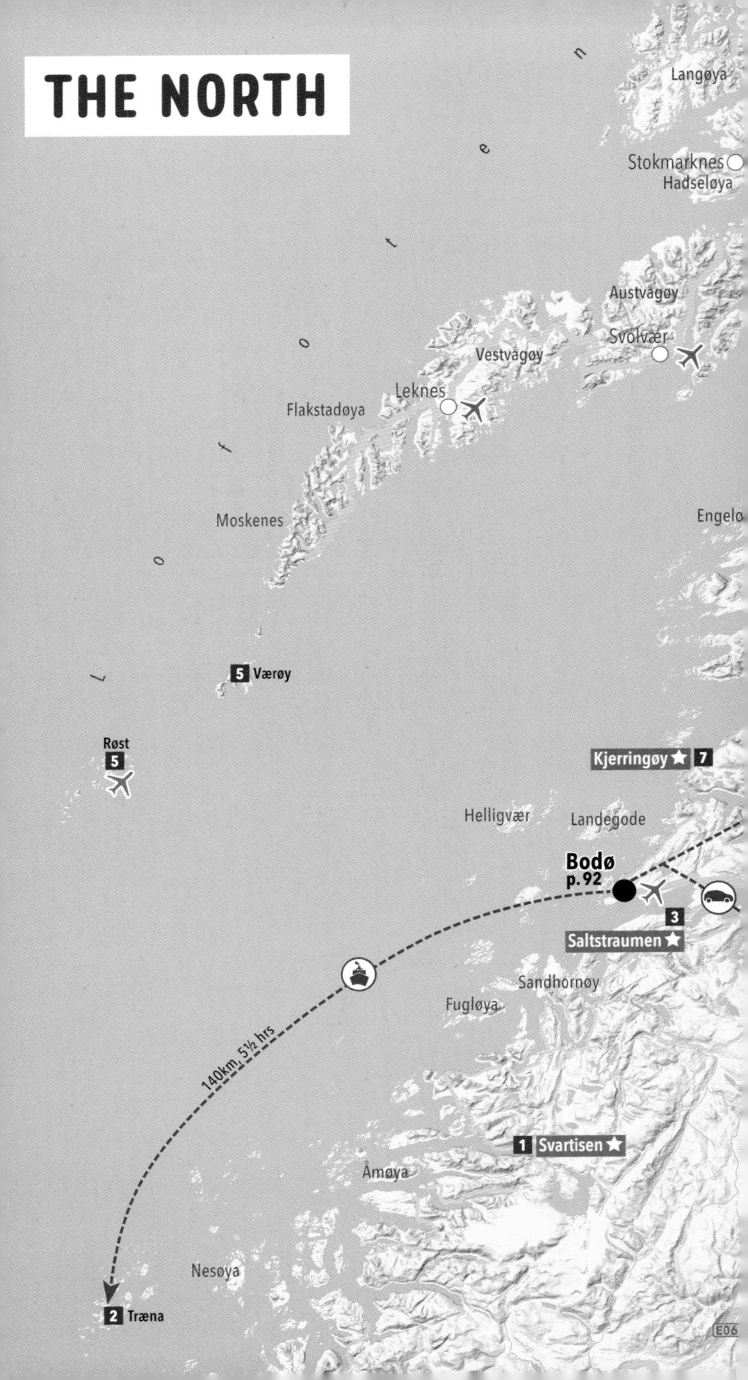

Langøya

Stokmarknes ○
Hadseløya

e

t

o

Austvågøy

Svolvær ○ ✈

Vestvågøy

Leknes ○ ✈

Flakstadøya

Moskenes

Engelo

f

o

l

5 Værøy

Røst
5 ✈

Kjerringøy ★ 7

Helligvær   Landegode

Bodø
p.92 ● ✈

3
Saltstraumen ★

🚢

Sandhornøy

Fugløya

140km, 5½ hrs

1 Svartisen ★

Åmøya

Nesøya

2 Træna

E06

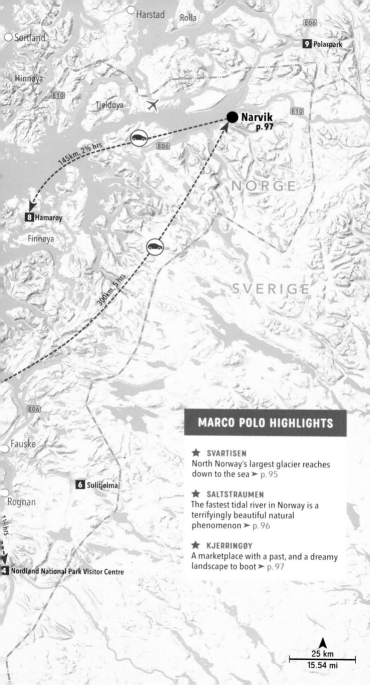

○ Harstad Rolla

○ Sortland

⊙ Polarpark **9**

Hinnøya

E10

Tjeldøya

✈

● **Narvik**
p. 97

145km, 2½ hrs 🚌

E06

NORGE

E10

8 Hamarøy

Finnøya

🚗

300km, 5 hrs

SVERIGE

E06

○ Fauske

6 Sulitjelma

○ Rognan

1½ hrs

4 Nordland National Park Visitor Centre

MARCO POLO HIGHLIGHTS

★ **SVARTISEN**
North Norway's largest glacier reaches down to the sea ➤ p. 95

★ **SALTSTRAUMEN**
The fastest tidal river in Norway is a terrifyingly beautiful natural phenomenon ➤ p. 96

★ **KJERRINGØY**
A marketplace with a past, and a dreamy landscape to boot ➤ p. 97

▲
25 km
15.54 mi

BODØ

(📖 F8) **It's said that the wind never stops blowing in Bodø (pop. 52,800). That may not be true, but this harbour town – Nordland's capital – is exposed to the Vestfjord.**

Only the 800m-high rugged peaks on Landego Island off the coast provide the people living in Bodø make up for that: when you take a stroll over the Moloveien on the seashore you will soon recognise that the Bodøværinger are warm-hearted and open-minded – their good humour typifies the town.

Bodø is also a major traffic junction. It is the terminus of the Nordland railway and the Hurtigruten ships dock directly opposite the station. Many

Extraterrestrials in Bodø? Wrap up warm when the Northern Lights are shining bright

a little protection from the icy storms that head in from the northwest.

Bodø received its town charter in 1860, but the German attack on 27 May 1940 destroyed the entire built-up area. That is why, today, many visitors think Bodø seems rather boring; there are not many buildings or residential areas worth visiting. But holidaymakers take a ferry to the Lofoten from here and express ships set off for the remote regions and islands on both sides of vast Vestfjord. Bodø is also the nursery of the Northern Atlantic cod and is the place to come if you want to eat a delicious dish of this fish.

SIGHTSEEING

BYMUSEET BODØ

The everyday life of Nordland's fish farmers and the Sami settlements are the main subjects in Nordland's oldest building (1903). Bodø's Iron Age silver treasure, which was found in 1919, is also kept here. *June–Aug daily 11am–4pm, otherwise Thu–Fri 11am–3pm, Sat/Sun noon–3pm | admission 80 NOK | Prinsens-gate 116 | nordlandsmuseet.no/bymuseet | ⏱ 1 hr*

NYHOLMEN KULTURHISTORISKE OMRÅDE (LIGHTHOUSE & ENTRENCHMENT)

The reconstructed entrenchment that protected the trading station at Hundholmen (later the town of Bodø) between 1810 and 1835 is on a small island just offshore. From the lighthouse, you'll have a fine view of Bodø and the surrounding area from the sea.

NORSK LUFTFARTSMUSEUM 😞

The history of Norwegian civil aviation and the air force, a flight simulator and the depiction of what happens when a plane takes off or lands: exciting impressions for young and old. *June–Aug daily 10am–6pm, otherwise Mon–Fri 10am–4pm, Sat/Sun 11am–5pm | admission 175 NOK, children 90 NOK | luftfartsmuseum.no | ⏱ 1 hr*

BODIN KIRKE

The stone church, built around 1240, lies directly on Saltfjord about 3km from the town centre. The richly decorated altarpiece from 1670 is especially noteworthy. The "Baroque organ" is younger as it is a replica made in 2003, but it makes an impressive sound. *Mid-June–late Aug Mon–Fri 10am–3pm | ⏱ 30 mins*

KEISERVARDEN

An easy, three-hour hike over the nearby hills will be rewarded with the most beautiful view over the Norwegian Sea to the Lofoten Wall. From 350m up, just below the treeline, you can watch the midnight sun sink until it barely touches the sea before rising again – provided that the summer weather is fine. Concerts are also held here during the *Nordland Music Festival. More information and hiking maps are available at the Turistinformasjon (visitbodo.com).*

EATING & DRINKING

LØVOLDS KAFETERIA

Reasonably priced Norwegian home-style cooking. The restaurant uses ingredients from the Arctic and serves large portions. If you want to try halibut, this is the place do it! *Tollbugta 9 | tel. 75 52 02 61 | lovoldskafeteria.no | £*

MELKEBAREN ☂

Don't let the name "The Milk Bar" fool you, because, in this coffee shop, milk is mainly an accompaniment for perfectly roasted and prepared coffee. They also serve croissants, cinnamon rings and ice cream. Watch the world go by outside the window, even in the pouring rain. *Storgata 16 | tel. 99 75 92 94 | £–££*

INSIDER TIP
Coffee & something sweet

SHOPPING

Seeing as it's always windy and sometimes quite cold, an entire street of shops in Bodø has been glazed over: you'll find everything you need in the *Glasshuset* in the town centre. Souvenirs, jewellery and useful articles made of (mostly local) stone, can be bought at *Bertnes Geo-Senter (bertnesgeosenter.no | around 8km east of Bodø).*

SPORT & ACTIVITIES

FISHING

Fishing is possible everywhere here. In the fjord and on the open sea, from the shore or from a boat. Salmon, cod and halibut of seemingly record size can be caught on *cutter trips on the Saltstraumen.* The size of the boat, length of the excursion and price vary according to the number of people taking part. *Info: Tuvsjyen AS (tel. 75 58 77 91 | tuvsjyen.com).*

NORDLANDSBADET 🏊

One of the loveliest water parks in Norway. There are various swimming pools and slides, whirlpools and corners where you can relax – and there's a spa area *(Mon–Thu 3–9pm, Fri/Sat noon–8pm, Sun until 6pm | admission 310 NOK)* with grottos, a herbal steam bath and Finnish sauna on the first floor. *Mon, Wed/Thu 3–9pm, Tue and Fri 6.30am–9pm, Sat/Sun 10am–6pm | admission 200 NOK, 10–15-year-olds 162 NOK, 3–9-year-olds 132 NOK | Plassmyrveien 11–15 | bodospektrum.no*

Your boat tour starts in Bodø and heads to the Saltstraumen tidal river

SEA EAGLE SAFARI

In the summer, Stella Polaris organise a daily trip at 4pm to the island of Landego to see Scandinavia's largest bird of prey in action. *Ferry 850 NOK | book at the Turistinformasjon (Tourist Information Office) (visit bodo.com) | departure from the Hurtigruten dock.*

FESTIVALS

NORDLAND MUSIKKFESTUKE

Every year, in the two weeks at the beginning of August, the sound of classical and jazz music can be heard over the sea in the Arctic air. The stage couldn't be more magical. *Tickets from 450 NOK | tel. 75 54 90 40 | musikk festuka.no*

AROUND BODØ

1 SVARTISEN ★

160km / 2 hrs 20 mins from Bodø to Braset resting area (by car via Fylkevei 17)

You can get very close to Norway's second-largest glacier if you approach it from the sea. *Engabreen*, a glacier snout that reaches down to the shore, is an especially popular tourist destination. In summer, small ships depart daily from the village of *Holand* on Road 17 for the glacier; visitors have to walk on the path for the last 3km to the ice or else they can rent a bicycle (rentals at the dock). Equipment for climbing the glacier is available on site. Info and bookings for glacier tours at *Rocks 'n Rivers (May–Sept | 1,200 NOK for 6 hrs | tel. 41 08 29 81 | rocksnrivers.no). ⊞ E–F 8–9*

2 TRÆNA

140km / 5½ hrs from Bodø (ship)

There are good reasons for visiting northern Norway's smallest community (pop. 500). Only very few of the almost 1,000 islands and islets near the Arctic Circle are inhabited, and the people here have all grown up with the sea. They're either fisherfolk or are involved in salmon farming and are happy to see any visitor who comes by. Even hobby anglers will be very successful in the fishing grounds between the islands, and the enormous puffin colony on the island of *Lovund* is a fascinating spectacle. At the beginning of

July, the *Træna Festival (3-day pass 2,055 NOK | trena.net)* takes place:

first-rate rock and pop from Norway, tent camps, fine seafood straight off the cutter, sun and rain are the ingredients that make this an unforgettable experience at the Arctic Circle. With only around 2,000 – mostly young – visitors, it's quite a cosy event. *Express ship from the centre (tickets from 705 NOK | reisnordland.no.)* F9

3 SALTSTRAUMEN ⭐

33km / 30 mins from Bodø (by car via Riksvei 80)

The most savage tidal river in the country is a gruesomely beautiful sight from afar. For six hours, vast quantities of water are forced through the 3km-long and only 150m-wide sound at almost 40kmh – you can hear the thundering force of nature from the bridge. Fisherfolk appreciate other qualities that this fjord entrance has to offer as it is here that the largest rock salmon in Europe are caught; the record is 22.7kg. If you want to experience the force of the current close up, you can hire a good boat for a fishing trip at *Saltstraumen Brygge (tel. 92 45 51 00 | sfc.no | 3 days from 3,100 NOK)* and book accommodation. F8

4 NORDLAND NATIONAL PARK VISITOR CENTRE

116km / 1 hr 40 mins from Bodø (via Riksvei 80 and E6)

This visitor centre has something for everyone, with its Norwegian and Sami art and the marvellous modern architecture that evokes the nature of the Nordland. In summer, there are regular campfires in the inner courtyard, inviting visitors to sit down for a while and enjoy the unparalleled atmosphere. *June–Aug daily noon–5pm | admission free | tel. 40 06 72 51 | nordlandsnaturen.no |* ⏱ *1 hr |* F8

5 RØST & VÆRØY

Røst 100km / 7 hrs, Værøy 85km / 4½ hrs from Bodø (by ferry from quay)

You can reach the bird islands of *Røst* and *Værøy* either in the 35-seat plane operated by Widerøe or by ferry from Bodø. The livelihood of the approximately 1,300 people who live on the islands depends on fish. The constant wind, mild winters and cool summers make it the perfect place for producing dried cod that is then exported to southern Europe. The cliffs on the south-west of the islands provide shelter for gigantic colonies of seabirds. A quarter of Norway's entire seabird population nests on the rocks of Røst – and that means around 2.5 million birds: puffins, gulls, cormorants and sea eagles. The tourist offices on the islands can give further information on boat trips to the bird rocks. E7

6 SULITJELMA

90km / 1½ hrs from Bodø (by car via Riksvei 80)

The former mining town of Sulitjelma, where copper was extracted between 1887 and 1991, lies at the end of Road 830, surrounded by mountain ranges and glaciers. The *Mining Museum (in summer, daily 11am–5pm | admission*

Anything else? An old shop in Kjerringøy

80 NOK) gives an overview of 100 years of mining. The oldest pit marks the beginning of the 800km *Nordkalottleden* walking trail, which also passes through Sweden and Finland. ⌘ F8

7 KJERRINGØY ★

42km / 1 hr from Bodø (by car via Road 834)

This traditional trading post with 15 buildings from the 19th century has an absolutely beautiful coastal setting on the vast Vestfjord. Here you will get a good impression of the everyday life led by the masters and their servants in a typical Norwegian merchant town in times gone by – you could almost be in a Knut Hamsun novel. The café *Markens Grøde (late July–late Aug)* only uses products from the

neighbouring organic farm. A hike from the Kjerringøy parsonage to *Middagshaugen* mountain is worthwhile, but don't forget to put on your hiking boots. *Mid-May–late Aug daily 11am–5pm, Sept–early May Sat 11.30am–3pm | admission 120 NOK | short.travel/nor17 |* ⊙ *1 hr |* ⌘ *F7*

NARVIK

(⌘ G6) **Some of the fiercest battles in World War II were fought in Narvik (pop. 21,500). The reason was the harbour's economic and strategic importance.**

Iron ore from the mines in Kiruna in Sweden is still shipped out of Narvik today. The gigantic loading wharfs are the dominating impression of a town that is located in a magnificent setting.

SIGHTSEEING

FJELLHEISEN (CABLE CAR)

If you decide to stay in town but still want to enjoy a fine view, the cable car *(fjellheisen)* can be recommended. It will whisk you up to an elevation of 656m in a mere seven minutes. When the sky is blue, the fjord and *fjell –* and sometimes the midnight sun – combine to create a breathtaking panorama. *June/July daily noon–midnight, Aug daily noon–7pm, Sept/Oct Fri 4–10pm, Sat 11am–6pm | return fare 235 NOK | ⏱ 1 hr*

NARVIK KRIGSMUSEUM

The battles for Narvik and its iron ore as well as the destruction of the town in World War II are documented in this museum. The exhibition is well worth seeing and will stay with you. *In summer daily 10am–6pm, otherwise shorter opening times | admission 130 NOK | directly on the Market Square | warmuseum.no | ⏱ 1 hr*

OFOTBANEN

The Ofot Railway, one of the most exciting stretches of track in Europe, runs between fjords and Arctic plateaus. Travelling on this train will give you some idea of the hardships endured by the migrant workers who built the line more than 100 years ago. *Visit Narvik (visitnarvik.com)* offers guided round-trip tours *(600 NOK)*. Head by train to Katterat up in the mountains, then hike 13km to Rombaksbotn at the end of the fjord with the same name, where a RIB boat will pick you up.

Fresh snow in Narvik – perfect for snowboarding

EATING & DRINKING

RALLAR'N PUB OG KRO

Rustic and somewhat loud in the evenings thanks to the live music, but a good place to get a solid meal at lunchtime. *Kongensgate 64 | in Quality Hotel Grand Royal | tel. 76 97 70 00 | short.travel/nor19 | ££*

SPORT & ACTIVITIES

Alpine sports are very popular between the fjord and *fjell*: Alpine World Cup races are even held in Narvik. The cable cars and lifts operate until late May. The ski centre is right in town, making the distance between your accommodation and the slopes short. Narvik is a favourite among snowboarders.

AROUND NARVIK

8 HAMARØY

145km / 2½ hrs from Narvik (by car via E6)

"The sky all open and clean; I stared into that clear sea…". This sentence in Knut Hamsun's book *Pan* was written during the many years he spent on the Hamarøy Peninsula. The community has a picturesque coastal setting surrounded by bizarre peaks. The *Hamsunsenteret (June–Aug daily 11am–6pm, otherwise shorter opening times | admission 130 NOK | Presteid | hamsunsenteret.no)* created by the American architect Steven Holl contains the most comprehensive exhibition on the life and work of the famous novelist. Stop at the *Tranøy fyr* lighthouse and build up your strength with fish soup or prawns. From here, you can enjoy an undisturbed view far into the distance. People who like to fish can also try to catch something fresh here. *F7*

9 POLARPARK

85km / 1 hr 20 mins from Narvik (by car via E6)

Norway's "National Predatory Animal Centre" lies north of Narvik in the Salangsdalen valley. The animal life includes elk, musk, oxen and reindeer as well as wolves, lynxes and brown bears. *June–Aug daily 10am–6pm | admission 260 NOK, children (3–15 years) 160 NOK, families 750 NOK | Bardu | polarpark.no | ⏱ 2 hrs | G6*

LOFOTEN & VESTERÅLEN

SPECTACULAR ISLANDS OF THE NORTH

What is so special about these islands? Is it the bright light in summer? Or the mighty Lofoten Wall which can be climbed late into the night? Or the splash of red from the old fishermen's houses, the sight of which may well elicit a romantic sigh?

Or perhaps it's the Arctic waves on the coast, known to surfers from around the world: surfing these waves in the ice-cold water of the North Atlantic is more daring challenge than sporting fun.

Small town, vast scenery: Reine is on Moskenes island, in the very south of Lofoten

Lofoten is not only cool, but it is also a cult spot, and shouldn't be missed if you're travelling to the north. Why would you deprive yourself of a fabulous whale safari or a boat tour on the stormy lake that runs from Andenes to Vesterålen, north of Lofoten? Both groups of islands provide the best opportunities to see (and photograph) rare animal species. In summary, this is the perfect place for (extreme) sports enthusiasts and nature lovers alike.

LOFOTEN & VESTERÅLEN

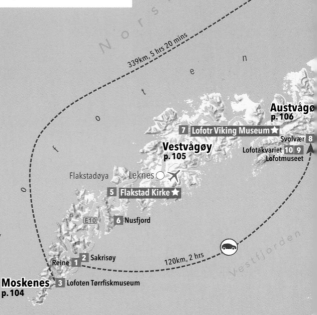

339km, 5 hrs 20 mins

120km, 2 hrs

Austvågø
p. 106

7 Lofotr Viking Museum ★

Svolvær 8

Vestvågøy
p. 105

Lofotakvariet 10 9
Lofotmuseet

Flakstadøya   Leknes

5 Flakstad Kirke ★

E10   6 Nusfjord

Reine 1 2 Sakrisøy

Moskenes
p. 104   3 Lofoten Tørrfiskmuseum

4 Moskenesstraumen

Norskehavet

Vestfjorden

12 Andenes ★

Aurora Spacecraft **13**

Andøya
p.108

82

128km 2 hrs

Langøya

Sortland

15 Akvakult i Vesterålen

Hurtigrutemuseet

Hinnøya

okmarknes
adseløya

11 Trollfjord ★

Hamarøy

Finnøya

Engeløya

Senja

Grytøya

Andørja

Harstad

Rolla

Tjeldøya

E10

Ofotfjorden

NORGE

SVERIGE

25 km
15.54 mi

MOSKENES

(□ E7) **Moskenes is the southernmost island of the Lofoten archipelago, which extends north from the giant Vestfjord.**

This area and its surroundings provide some of the most beautiful viewing points and fishing spots on the islands.

SIGHTSEEING

1 REINE

Reine (pop. 1,000) is picturesque in the true sense of the word, with its pointed mountain peaks and clear water. The smell of fish drying on the racks, which is typical of Lofoten, is everywhere here from March to autumn.

2 SAKRISØY

The more than 100-year-old yellow and white cabins *(rorbuer)* in this fishing settlement form a fantastic contrast to the surrounding mountains. These huts, resting on stilts, used to form the fishing quarter in the fishing season. Today, they provide accommodation.

3 LOFOTEN TØRRFISKMUSEUM

Å is a living museum village. The production of dried fish has a long tradition on the Lofoten and here you can learn about it step by step in the buildings of a traditional fish factory. Accommodation in the village *(lofotenferie.com)*. June–late Aug

INSIDER TIP
Fishy business

Mon–Sat 11am–4pm, otherwise by appointment | admission 60 NOK | end of the E10 | ⏱ 1 hr

EATING & DRINKING

HOLMEN LOFOTEN/KITCHEN ON THE EDGE OF THE WORLD

Experience the rugged Arctic with all your senses: Valentine Warner is experimental, looking for new tastes with top chefs and bartenders from all over the world – it's an experience for your palate. *Sørvågen | tel. 93 44 23 01 | holmenlofoten.no | £££*

SPORT & ACTIVITIES

Bicycles and boats are available for rent at almost all hotels and accommodation. You can fish from the shore or from a boat.

AROUND MOSKENES

4 MOSKENESSTRAUMEN

Approx. 20km from Reine (boat tours)

The strait lies between the southern tip of the Lofoten, Lofotodden, and the island of Værøy. There are guided walks to the legendary maelstrom in summer, made famous by Edgar Allan Poe. *Boat tours from Reine, including at Aqua Lofoten Coast Adventure (April–Sept from 10am, July from 1pm | duration approx. 2 hrs | 1,195 NOK | aqualofoten.no).* □ E7

From this high up, Reine looks like a model village

5 FLAKSTAD KIRKE ★

30km / 35 mins from Reine (by car via E10)

Boats and water are the main themes here. This much-restored church was originally built from cargo driftwood, but many of its furnishings are now missing. The model of a fishing boat in the centre of the church reminds visitors of the community's maritime roots. 🕐 *1 hr* | 🗺 *E7*

6 NUSFJORD

41km / 50 mins from Reine (by car via E10)

This picturesque fishing village on the Vestfjord is on the island of Flakstadøy. Most of the *rorbuer* (cabins) date from the 19th century and have been restored and turned into holiday accommodation. *nusfjord.no* | 🗺 *E7*

VESTVÅGØY

(🗺 E7) **The runway at Leknes Airport is one of the shortest in Norway at just 1,070m. So when you land, you are straight into the thick of it.**

Leknes (pop. 3,500) is the centre of the island and community of Vestvågøy. The post-war architecture has little charm, but the surroundings of the small town have a lot to offer – also for fans of the Vikings.

SIGHTSEEING

7 LOFOTR VIKING MUSEUM ★

This is how the Vikings lived: the museum to the north of Leknes has an impressive reconstruction of the largest Viking house ever found at 83m long. The Vikings held political and religious meetings in the "guildhall". Today, a fire blazes in the hall and

A mighty sea eagle in its natural habitat on Lofoten

visitors can sit and rest on furs. *June–mid-Aug daily 10am–7pm, otherwise shorter opening times | admission 225 NOK | lofotr.no | ⏱ 1 hr*

EATING & DRINKING

SKJÆBRYGGA

Excellent fish dishes are served here directly on the quay in Stamsund. *Only in summer | tel. 76 05 46 00 | livelofoten.com | ££*

SHOPPING

LOFOTEN DESIGN

In the Norwegian Sea, on the neighbouring island of Flakstadøy, you'll find the village of Vikten where Åse and Åsvar Tangrand have a glass-blowing and pottery workshop. The two artists give their imagination free rein – much to the delight of the visitors. *April–May daily 10am–4pm, June–Aug 10am–7pm | admission to workshop and "Potter's Tower" 20 NOK | glasshyttavikten.no*

AUSTVÅGØY

(📖 F6–7) **For many, Austvågøy is just a springboard to areas on the Lofoten considered more attractive, but it is actually charming in its own right.**

The mountainous island resembles an Alpine region and there's a reason that the 671m-high *Skottinden* has the nickname "Matterhorn of the Lofoten". Alongside panoramic views and endless sea beaches, you'll also find countless hiking routes and places to climb.

SIGHTSEEING

🅱 SVOLVÆR

The capital of the Lofoten lies beneath the Svolvægeita mountain (called the Solvær Goat because of its two horns). The value of the landed cod, herring and farmed salmon makes Solvær (pop. 4,700) one of the most important fishing ports in northern Norway.

The racks used for drying the fish, which can also be seen on the smaller islands, are clear evidence of this.

9 LOFOTMUSEET

The regional museum was established on the remains of Vågar, the only northern Norwegian town in the Middle Ages. The main building is a typical grand merchant's house from 1815; in the other houses the main focus of the exhibition is the everyday life of everyday people. And, of course, you'll see plenty of boats and fishing equipment. *In summer daily 10am–6pm, otherwise shorter opening times | admission 110 NOK | Kabelvåg, Ortsteil Storvågan | lofotmuseet.no | ⊙ 1 hr*

10 LOFOTAKVARIET 🐵

Mainly animals that live in the Norwegian Sea swim in the pools of the Lofoten Aquarium near Svolvær. Children are particularly fond of the sea otters and seals. *June–Aug daily 10am–6pm, otherwise Sun–Fri 11am–3pm | admission adults 140 NOK, children 90 NOK, families 400 NOK | Kabelvåg | Storvågen district | lofotakvariet.no | ⊙ 1½ hrs*

EATING & DRINKING

BØRSEN SPISERI

The seafood restaurant (reservation required!) is located in the Spiseri resort, which has 38 one- to three-bedroom *rorbuer* (cabins). *Gunnars Bergs vei 2 | tel. 76 06 99 31 | svinoya.no | ££*

SHOPPING

SKANDINAVISK HØYFJELLSUTSTYR

In case you forget something you need for your trekking holiday: the experts in this shop know everything there is to know about the land and water in the vicinity and can provide you with all the necessary equipment. *Håkon Kyllingsmarks gate 3 | Svolvær*

SPORT & ACTIVITIES

FISHING

In summer, cutters and tourist boats take hobby anglers out to sea. Anybody can participate in the *World Cod Fishing Championship* at the end of March. *lofoten.info*

KAISER ROUTE

From Svolvær through the countryside of the northern Lofoten: the 220km Kaiser route will take you to remote places that are hardly ever reached by car – along Raftsund with the world-famous Trollfjord and back to the start. Cycling is most enjoyable in the evening. If you're lucky, harbour porpoises or even killer whales might accompany you on your way through Raftsund. *lofoten-online.de*

INSIDER TIP
Cycle with sea creatures

SEAL & SEA EAGLE SAFARI

Sea eagle and seal safaris (895 NOK) with a solid RIB boat depart from Henningsvær and last one and a half hours. If the weather is good, the three-hour midnight tours to the western side of the Lofoten (1,095 NOK) are a dream come true. You get to experience the open sea and the jagged mountain peaks even more intensely in the light of the midnight sun. *Lofoten Opplevelser | tel. 90 58 14 75 | lofo ten-opplevelser.no*

AROUND AUSTVÅGØY

⑪ TROLLFJORD ★

Approx. 15km from Svolvær (by boat)
Experience the monumental natural beauty of the Trollfjord. Large tourist boats have to turn around in this extremely narrow sidearm of Raftsund. While this is happening, passengers admire the rocky shore rising straight up to the skies and the fascinating play of light on the water. *Boat tours from Svolvær, including from Lofoten Explorer (duration approx. 2 hrs | 945 NOK | lofoten-explorer.no). 🖽 F6*

ANDØYA

(🖽 F5–6) **The island of Andøya belongs both to the Lofoten and the Vesterålen archipelagos. The main inhabitants are fisherfolk and those working on the military base there.**

With a bit of luck, you will see whales and seals from the coast. A new, futuristic whale centre called *The Whale* is set to open in Andenes in 2025.

SIGHTSEEING

⑫ ANDENES ★

Although surrounded by a wall of mountains and snow-white beaches, the main town (pop. 2,700) on the island of Andøya lies at the mercy of the blue-green Norwegian Sea. Andenes lives off its whale-watching tours (see Sport & Activities, below). If you prefer to stay on land, the kilometres of sandy beaches are a great place for walking. You can head for the *lighthouse* and climb the 148 steps to the top for a spectacular view over the sea.

⑬ AURORA SPACECRAFT 😯

Did you know that this of all places is the centre of Norwegian space travel? But not only that: you can also learn about the infinite expanse of space and find out more about the Northern Lights. *"Space mission" from 300 NOK, children and young people (10–16 years) 300 NOK, it's best to buy tickets online | spaceshipaurora.no | ⏱ 1 hr*

EATING & DRINKING

ARRESTEN

In the rugged surroundings of Andenes, you'll find this restaurant, like a warm, cosy oasis. Of course, they serve fish. The most popular dish is fish and chips. If you want something traditional, try the clipfish carpaccio – it doesn't get more Norwegian than that! *Prinsensgate 6 | Andenes | FB: arresten.no | ££*

In their element: orcas are very much at home in the Norwegian Sea

SHOPPING

ALVELAND BUTIKK & CAFÉ

The pleasant smell of home-made soap will welcome you at the entrance. Soap maker Rita sources her ingredients – such as cloudberries, nettles and goat's milk – on the island itself. There's also a café serving home-baked cakes. *June–Aug Thu–Sun 11am–4pm | Dverberg | alveland.no*

SPORT & ACTIVITIES

WHALE-WATCHING

Excursions to the continental shelf start from the whale centre in Andenes (see above). Sperm whales up to 18m in length come here in summer and often emerge for photos. *20 June–20 Aug daily 11am, noon, 4pm and 5pm | from harbour | duration 2–4 hrs | 1,240 NOK | tel. 76 11 56 00 | whale safari.com*

AROUND ANDØYA

🔢 HURTIGRUTEMUSEET

128km / 2 hrs from Andenes (by car via Fylkesvei 82)

Richard With, the "father" of the Hurtigruten, came from Stokmarknes and that's precisely where the 1956 ship *MS Finnmarken* has dropped anchor – as a museum. *Summer daily 9am–6pm | admission 225 NOK | hurtigrutemuseet.no | ⊙ 1 hr | ⊞ F6*

🔢 AKVAKULTUR I VESTERÅLEN 👪

128km / 2 hrs from Andenes (by car via Fylkesvei 82)

In Blokken, you can see a fish farm up close. The guided boat trip out into the water involves a salmon tasting from the company's own fish. *Mon–Fri 10am–4pm | advanced booking essential, 150 NOK, children: 60 NOK | tel. 95 88 18 22 | akvakulturivesteralen. no | ⊙ 1 hr | ⊞ F6*

TROMS

THE ENCHANTING ARCTIC

Don't presume that it's all solitude and loneliness up here – it just depends which way you're facing! If you look north, it's true, there aren't many people; but if you look elsewhere, you'll be happy to find that you're not alone.

Arriving at the university city of Tromsø feels like landing at a large student party. Regardless of whether there's midnight sun or it's a polar night, there are young people everywhere, heading to bars

A spectacular coastal view: this small lighthouse has a front-row seat

and restaurants after work or college. Those who study here love the charm of this "Paris of the North", as polar explorers once called it.

If you travel a few kilometres outside of the city, you'll get a completely different picture. The low treeline means the landscape is fairly barren. Occasionally, rivers wend their way like narrow arteries through the landscape, with the odd sandy beach and fishing village on the islands further out.

TROMS

MARCO POLO HIGHLIGHTS

★ **TROMSØ**
In the summer, the sun shines at midnight and nobody feels like going to bed ➤ p. 114

★ **LYNGSALPEN**
Off-piste ski tours in magical snowy scenery ➤ p. 117

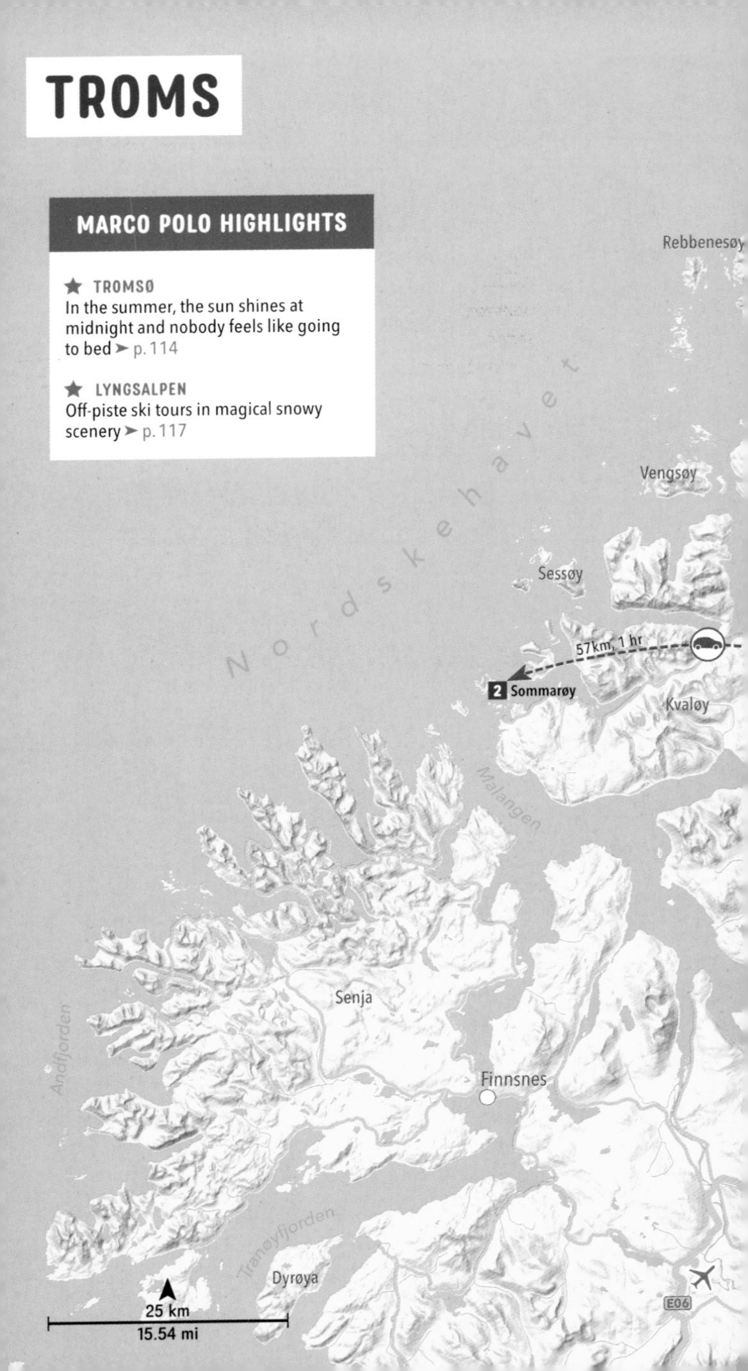

Rebbenesøy
Nordskehavet
Vengsøy
Sessøy
57km, 1 hr
2 Sommarøy
Kvaløy
Malangen
Senja
Andfjorden
Finnsnes
Tranøyfjorden
Dyrøya
E06
25 km
15.54 mi

Nordkvaløya

Fugløya

Helgøy

Vanna

Arnøy

Lopphavet

Kagen

Ringvassøy

Reinøy

Uløya

Grøtsundet

Ullsfjorden

Lyngen

E06

✈ **Tromsø** ★
p.114

70 km, 1 hr

🚗

E08

3 Lyngsalpen ★

Balsfjorden

E08

1 Vollan Gjestestue

N O R G E

E06

E08

S U O M I

S V E R I G E

TROMSØ

(□ G5) **A "cool" city!** ★ **Tromsø (pop. 78,000) is a vibrant light illuminating the country's dark north.**

Boasting a lively music scene and animated pub culture, the city's nightlife attracts a predominately young crowd of students from the world's most northern university. Tromsø can stay covered in snow until mid-May; then the midnight sun appears between 23 May and 23 July. Enjoy spending the long nights beneath starry skies – just wrap up warm.

FJELLHEISEN (CABLE CAR)

The cable cars, known as "Seal" and "Polar Bear", take you up to the top of *Mount Storsteinen* (421m) in just four minutes. The views of the city and the mouth of the polar sea will literally take your breath away. *Daily 9am–midnight, every 30 mins | 320 NOK | fjellheisen.no | ⏱ 1 hr*

ISHAVSKATEDRALEN

The glass "Arctic Ocean Cathedral" can be spotted from the city centre – the best way to get there is to walk across the city bridge *(Tromsø bru)*. The gigantic glass mosaic on the east wall is especially impressive as are the *Midnight Sun Concerts* – the acoustics and the sound of the organ are

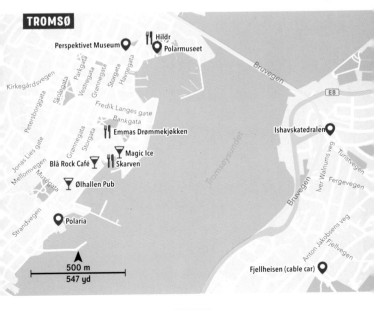

TROMSØ

Perspektivet Museum

Hildr
Polarmuseet

Bruvegen

Kirkegårdsvegen

Petersborggata
Skolegata
Parkgata
Vestregata
Grønnegata
Storgata
Havnegata

E8

Fredik Langes gate
Bankgata

Jonas Lies gate
Mellomvegen
Muégata
Grønnegata
Storgata

Emmas Drømmekjøkken

Ishavskatedralen

Magic Ice

Blå Rock Café
Skarven

Tromsøysundet

Iver Walnums veg
Turrstvegen
Fergevegen

Ølhallen Pub

Bruvegen

Strandvegen

Polaria

Anton Jakobsens veg
Fjellvegen

500 m
547 yd

Fjellheisen (cable car)

The Polar Museum at Tromsø tells you about expeditions in the Arctic Ocean

amazing. *May–Aug Mon–Sat 9am–6pm, Sun 1–6pm | admission 55 NOK | ishavskatedralen.no | ⊙ 45 mins*

PERSPEKTIVET MUSEUM 🐷

How difficult was life here on the edge of the Arctic Circle? How important was fishing and how did the traders live? Take time to look at the exhibits in this listed building and you will come to a better understanding of northern Norway. *Tue–Fri 10am–4pm, Sat/Sun 11am–5pm | admission 50 NOK | Storgata 95 | perspektivet.no | ⊙ 1 hr*

POLARMUSEET

Norway's polar history, polar expeditions, and seal and polar bear hunting are the themes in the Polar Museum that has been set up in the old harbour warehouses. *In summer daily 9am–5pm, otherwise shorter opening times | admission 100 NOK | Søndre* *Tollbodgata 11 | polarmuseum.no | ⊙ 1½ hrs*

POLARIA 😋

This fantastic information and adventure centre in Tromsø includes a wide-screen cinema with a film about the polar regions, as well as an aquarium, a seal pool, and exhibitions on polar research. *In summer daily 10am–5pm, otherwise 10am–4pm | admission: adults 210 NOK, children 105 NOK | Hjalmar Johansensgate 12 | polaria.no | ⊙ 1½ hrs*

EATING & DRINKING

EMMAS DRØMMEKJØKKEN

Emma, whose real name is Anne Brit, serves an authentic and legendary fish gratin. Once you have

INSIDER TIP
Famous gratin

tried the dish, you can cook it yourself by following the recipe online. *Kirkegata 8 | tel. 77 63 77 30 | emmas drommekjokken.no | ££*

HILDR

You should absolutely try the *skreiviche* from *Hildr*, a take on the South American *ceviche*, served with *skrei (codfish)*. Expect explosions of flavour. The place has a cosy and homely atmosphere. *Skippergata 11 | tel. 94 09 62 47 | hildr.no | ££*

SKARVEN

The perfect place for a long evening. Why not begin in the *Biffhuset (££)* steak restaurant or in the *Arctandria (£££)* fish restaurant, continue in the *Kroa (£)* pub and finish up at the cocktail bar in the basement. *Strandtorget 1 | tel. 77 60 07 20 | skarven.no*

SHOPPING

The light of the north is evident in the artistic products created at the *Blåst* glass-blowing workshop *(Peder Hansensgate 4 | blaast.no)*. *Wabi Sabi (Peder Hansens gate 4B | wabisabi.no)* makes delightful items of jewellery in raw Scandinavian style.

The wool sold in *Snarby Strikkes tudio (Storgata 90)*, from Raumaull, Sandnes Garn and the Hillesvåg wool mill, is also a favourite of Tromsø-born fashion designer Nina Skarra, who now works in New York.

SPORT & ACTIVITIES

Husky or reindeer sleigh rides, whale-spotting safaris, Northern Lights expeditions or snowboarding tours are all once-in-a-lifetime experiences

You'll never forget a trip to see the Northern Lights

and can be booked online at *lyngs fjord.com*.

At *Tromsø Arctic Reindeer (30 mins from the town centre | tromsoarctic reindeer.com)* you can trace the lives of the indigenous Sami people.

NIGHTLIFE

BLÅ ROCK CAFÉ

Occasional live bands; DJs on Sundays. Happy hour is Monday 10.30pm–2am. *Strandgata 14–16 | blarock.no*

MAGIC ICE

Ice bars are popping up all over Europe, but this one in Tromsø has all the Arctic charm. Ice carvings depict Norwegian polar stories, which you can look at while enjoying a cool drink until you get icicles on the end of your nose. *Kaiagata 4 | tickets from 255 NOK | tel 41 30 10 50 | magicice.no*

ØLHALLEN PUB

Beer lovers have 67 varieties to choose from in the city's oldest pub. Definitely try *Mack Øl*, the only beer brewed in Tromsø. *Storgata 4 | mack.no/olhallen*

AROUND TROMSØ

1 VOLLAN GJESTESTUE

70km / 1 hr from Tromsø (by car via E8)

Voted by Norway's truck drivers as the best motorway stop in the country. The restaurant, at the junction of the E6

and E8, serves Arctic dishes made with regional ingredients. *Nordkjosbotn | tel. 77 72 23 00 | vollangjestestue. no | ££ | ⊞ H5*

2 SOMMARØY

60km / 1 hr from Tromsø (by car via Fylkesvei 862)

The drive from Tromsø along the south coast of the gigantic Kvaløya Island towards the west is an excursion into the fertile agricultural region of Troms and to the beautiful island of Sommarøy. Crystal-clear water, white beaches and flowering front gardens: many of the locals in Tromsø head here on sunny days for good reason! ⊞ G5

3 LYNGSALPEN ★

77km / 1¾ hrs from Tromsø to Lyngseidet (by car via E8 and Fylkesvei 91)

The snowy Arctic landscape feels as vast as Alaska and Greenland and is great for off-piste skiing and fans of extreme sports. Far from the ski-lift crowds and cabins, the adventurous among you will appreciate the untouched deep ski slopes. As you descend, you'll be able to see the Lyngen fjord at the foot of the mountains. ⊞ H5

FINNMARK

Icy winds meet open harbours, raging rivers flow into majestic fjords, and thousands of peaceful mountain lakes are besieged by myriad mosquitoes. This is Finnmark: 48,000km² and surrounded by the inhospitable coastline of the Arctic Ocean. The interior is characterised by a barren high plateau where tens of thousands of reindeer fight to survive in winter.

The 76,000 people who live in Finnmark live in close proximity to nature. Temperatures range from 30°C above to 50°C below zero. In

Hammerfest: the northernmost city in the world

winter, the houses are battered by storms, while in summer people bask in the sun on the beautiful sandy beaches and – from time to time – cool off in the Arctic Ocean; the water can be as warm as 14°C.

In Alta, the midnight sun shines from 16 May to 26 July and even a few days longer at the North Cape.

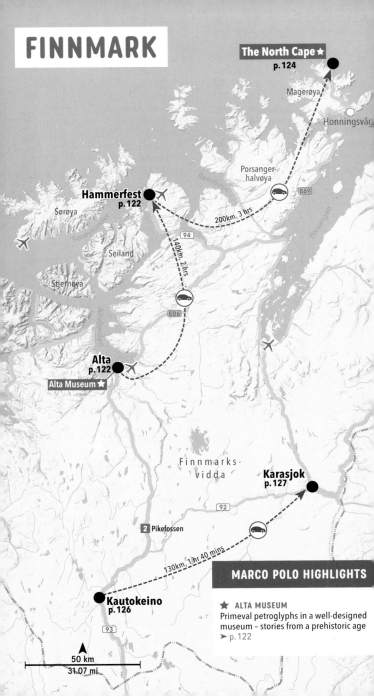

FINNMARK

The North Cape ★
p. 124

Magerøya

Honningsvåg

Porsanger-
halvøya

200km, 3 hrs

Hammerfest
p. 122

Sørøya

Seiland

Stjernøya

94

140km, 2 hrs

E06

Alta
p. 122

Alta Museum ★

Finnmarks-
vidda

Karasjok
p. 127

92

2 Pikefossen

130km, 1 hr 40 mins

Kautokeino
p. 126

93

MARCO POLO HIGHLIGHTS

★ **ALTA MUSEUM**
Primeval petroglyphs in a well-designed
museum – stories from a prehistoric age
➤ p. 122

50 km
31.07 mi

ALTA

(□ K2) **Alta (pop. 21,000) lies on the southern shore of the mighty Altafjord and is the largest town in Finnmark.**

The Arctic University of Norway has a campus here, and there is also some industry as well as quarries. The Altaelva salmon river runs down from Finnmarksvidda through Alta Canyon before flowing into Altafjord.

SIGHTSEEING

ALTA MUSEUM ★

What drove the first people to the northern edge of Europe? What did they live off and what did they believe in? The *helleristninger* (rock drawings), which are up to 7,000 years old, provide the answers. The 15km-long prehistoric comic strip includes over 6,000 drawings of countless animals, hunting scenes and ancient legends. The exhibitions on the prehistory of Finnmark are also worth seeing in the *Alta Museum. Early June–late Aug daily 9am–7pm, otherwise shorter opening times | admission 135 NOK | alta.museum.no | ⊙ 2 hrs*

EATING & DRINKING

DU VERDEN

The atmosphere here is rustic but urban: benches lined with reindeer fur and creative Nordic cuisine. Their dish of king prawns with chimichurri sauce is impressive. *Markedsgata 21 | tel. 45 90 82 13 | duverden.no/alta | ££–£££*

SPORT & ACTIVITIES

ALTA CANYON

It isn't easy to find your way to northern Europe's largest canyon, but it is well worth the effort. From *Gargia Fjellstue (gargia-fjellstue.norway-hotel. com)*, drive 11km to Sautso and then another 4km on the old state road *(gravel road)*. Park your car at the highest point, *Beskades*, and follow the hiking route marked with a red "T" for about 7km to the end of the 10km-long canyon. Make sure you pack appropriate clothing and mosquito spray! *Description at ut.no/tur/2.5967.*

HALDDETOPPEN

The hike to the peak of *Haldde Mountain* (904m) starts near *Kåfjord* (20km to the west of Alta on the E6). In 1898, the first Northern Lights observatory was established here. The climb requires fitness, but you'll be rewarded with a magnificent view over Altafjord.

HAMMERFEST

(□ K1) **Congratulations: you've reached the most northern city in the world!**

Fridtjof Nansen started his expeditions from its ice-free harbour. Today, the offshore industry shapes the city: the gas from the enormous "Snow White" field in the Barents Sea is processed in the refinery near Hammerfest (pop. 11,200) and provides the whole country with jobs and prosperity.

The rock carvings at the Alta Museum tell exciting stories

SIGHTSEEING

GJENREISNINGSMUSEET

This museum provides a graphic description of the destruction wreaked on Hammerfest during World War II and the efforts the Finnmarkingers had to undertake in order to rebuild it. *In summer daily 10am–4pm, otherwise Mon–Fri 9am–3pm, Sat/Sun 11am–2pm | admission 80 NOK | Kirkegata 21 | kystmuseene.no | ⏱ 1 hr*

MERIDIAN COLUMN

It's precisely 2,820km from this point to the Black Sea – the Meridian line shows you the way. The monument was erected in 1854 to commemorate the first survey of the globe.

EATING & DRINKING

NIRI SUSHI & DINNER

The world's most northerly sushi restaurant serves exciting creations. The signature dish is sushi with reindeer meat. *Storgata 22 | tel. 45 50 02 00 | nirihammerfest.no | ££–£££*

SHOPPING

Northern Lights soap and brightly coloured gloves can be found at *Vi4 (Kirkegata 8)*. It's also worth having a look at *Sirkka (Storgata 28)*, but you may need your credit card for its tempting jewellery, fashion and interior items.

THE NORTH CAPE

(📖 L1) **The ⭐ North Cape is not, in fact, the northernmost point in Europe, but it is still unforgettable. The 307m-high plateau on the island of Magerøy is 2,163km from Oslo.**

You reach the island through a 6.8km-long tunnel and, 45 minutes later, you arrive at the North Cape.

A memorial to witches in Varanger: remembering dark times

There are restaurants, souvenirs, a panorama bar and a small ecumenical chapel in the gigantic *North Cape Hall*. But the real drama at latitude 71°10′21″ is performed on the northern horizon from May to July if no fog or cloud veils the midnight sun. In summer, you won't find yourself alone here even in the middle of the night.

SIGHTSEEING

GJESVÆRSTAPPAN

You should try to get a close-up view of this bird rock and the spectacle performed by cormorants, puffins, **INSIDER TIP** *Feathered chaos*
seagulls and sea eagles. Tours are offered by *Gjesvær Turistsenter (3 tours daily in summer) | 890 NOK per person | tel. 41 61 39 83 | birdsafari.com)* and *Roald Berg (daily | 780 NOK per person | Gjesvær | tel. 95 03 77 22 | stappan.no)🕐 2 hrs*

KIRKEPORTEN

The hike to the "church door" rock is not very strenuous. From here, you have a fabulous view over the Norwegian Sea and towards the North Cape. *Starting point near Kirkeporten Camping in Skarsvåg*

VARANGER

(📖 M–N 1–2) **There are no trees and no green, only a lot of rocks and boulders on the ⭐ Varanger Peninsula.**

Tana Bru is the hub of East Finnmark. This is where you cross the River Tana, whose reputation is exceptional among salmon anglers. Road 890 leads to the Barents Sea, which is near *Berlevåg* (135km) and *Båtsfjord* (108km). Stay on Road 890 – the last 33km, the *Arctic Ocean Road* between Kongsfjord and Berlevåg, are breathtaking: storms, ice and saltwater have eroded the rocks and you'll see sandy terraces between them.

Vadsø (pop. 5,500, 66km) and *Vardø,* (pop. 1,900, 141km) are melting pots of many cultures. In the 18th and 19th centuries, the Kven people came from Finland and sought their luck as farmers, fishers and miners.

SIGHTSEEING

VADSØ MUSEUM (ESBENSGÅRDEN)

Here the culture of the Finnish-Norwegians (the Kvens) is fostered and passed on. The collections are displayed in a patrician house built in 1850 and a typical Kvene estate. *Mid-June–mid-Aug daily 11am–6pm | admission 100 NOK | Grensen 1 | Vadsø | varangermuseum.no | ⏲ 1 hr*

STEILNESET MINNESTED (WITCHES' MEMORIAL) 🐦

Art on the Arctic Ocean. On a strip of land at the edge of Vardø, you can walk through a 100m-long memorial designed by Swiss architect Peter Zumthor and visit the mini museum with the *Burning Chair* by the French-American sculptor Louise Bourgeois; both works commemorate the witch hunts of the 17th century. *Freely accessible | free admission | short.travel/nor13 | ⏲ 45 mins*

VARDØHUS FESTNING 🐦

This one-time defence complex in Vardø, built between 1734 and 1738 and guarded by an officer and four soldiers, is today an open-air museum. *Freely accessible. Military salutes Mon–Sat noon, Sun 1pm. Daily 8–9pm | admission free | Festningsgaten 20 | ⏲ 45 mins*

HAMNINGBERG

This fishing village, which was spared from the ravages of World War II, is only inhabited in summer. The drive is worth it: 35km from Vardø with a moonlike landscape on the left-hand side and the Arctic Ocean on the right. You'll be able to make out traces of movements in the earth's crust above the beautiful beaches.

INSIDER TIP
Journey to end all journeys

EATING & DRINKING

HAVHESTEN RESTAURANT

Do you want reindeer meat? Or kamchatka crabs? They taste best directly by the sea when it's sunny on the peninsula of Ekkerøy, 15km east of Vadsø. *Late June–mid-Aug | tel. 90 50 60 80 | ekkeroy.no | ££*

AROUND VARANGER

■ SØR-VARANGER

140km / 2 hrs from Tana Bru to Kirkenes (by car via E6)

After a long trip to the east, the E6 ends in *Kirkenes* (pop. 3,500). Here, the *Varanger Museum (varanger museum.no)* shows how the region was affected by World War II. If you prefer something more active, don't miss a fun *husky tour (from 2,000 NOK | prebooking online recommended | snowhotelkirkenes.com)*. The restless, four-legged speedsters with electric blue eyes fly with you through the countryside, in the winter with sleds, in the summer with a wagon.

The western edge of the Siberian Taiga called *Pasvik valley*, a national park, lies to the south of the town. A dense primeval forest with a great variety of flora makes for good hiking, but you should be careful – this is brown bear country. From *Height 96*, 40km south from Kirkenes, you can look over to Nikel in Russia. The *Skogfoss Waterfall* is only 50m from the Russian border. In the south of the national park, a heap of stones shows where Russia, Finland and Norway meet (5km from the end of the road in *Noatun*). ⬚ *M–N3*

KAUTOKEINO

(⬚ *K3*) **Kautokeino (pop. almost 3,000), the Sami's capital, lies around 130km south of Alta.**

It has a Sami theatre and Sami university, and the major Sami festival is

On your marks: reindeer races at the Easter Festival in Kautokeino

held here at Easter *(samieasterfestival. com)*, with family parties, concerts, theatre, artwork, and reindeer and snow-scooter races.

SIGHTSEEING

JUHLS' SILVERGALLERY

This silversmiths' workshop is the life work of two artists who have united Sami traditions with modern art and who create in silver their interpretations of the landscapes and people of Finnmark. *In summer daily 9am–8pm, otherwise 9am–6pm | free tours | juhls. no*

EATING & DRINKING

THON HOTEL KAUTOKEINO

The rustic wooden building fits perfectly into the countryside with an elegant interior in warm colours. Sami specialities grace the menu of the hotel restaurant *Biedjovággeluodda 2 | tel. 78 48 70 00 | thonhotels.no | £££*

AROUND KAUTOKEINO

☑ PIKEFOSSEN

44km / 35 mins from Kautokeino (by car via E45)

North of Kautokeino, this magnificent waterfall plummets down towards Alta. There's a rest area right beside the road and you can pitch up near the river.

KARASJOK

(□ L3) **This community in the middle of Finnmarksvidda has only 2,700 inhabitants, but is the political centre of Samiland.**

It is the site of the Sami parliament (Sameting) and is the heart of the traditional Sami territory. Karasjok is only 18km from the Finnish border and this makes it an important junction on the *Nordkalotte (Cap of the North)*.

SIGHTSEEING

KARASJOK GAMLE KIRKE

The Old Church, built in 1807, can be seen from far away; it's the only building in Karasjok that survived World War II. *In summer daily 8am–9pm | ◷ 20 mins*

SAMISK KUNSTNERSENTER

Arts and crafts as well as paintings by Sami artists sold in a bright and peaceful building. *Tue–Fri 10am–4pm, Sat/ Sun 11am–4pm | free admission | Suomageaidnu 14 | samidaidda guovddas.no | ◷ 1 hr*

SHOPPING

BOBLE GLASHYTTE

The northernmost glassworks on earth. The everyday objects are characterised by their simplicity and subdued colours while the artworks created by the owner Tonje Tunold have much more daring shapes and colours. *Sápmi Park | bobleglass.no*

DISCOVERY TOURS

Want to get under the skin of this country? Then our discovery tours are the ideal guide – they provide advice on which sights to visit, tips on where to stop for that perfect holiday snap, a choice of the best places to eat and drink, and suggestions for fun activities.

❶ THROUGH THE FJORDS

- ➤ Have your breath taken away at Preikestolen
- ➤ Blustery moments at Låtefossen waterfall
- ➤ At an impasse over Hardangerfjord

📍	Stavanger		Sognefjord
→	460km	🚗	2 days (12 hrs total driving time)

ℹ Cost: £180 (fuel, tolls, ferry crossings)
What to pack: hiking gear (hiking boots, rain gear, sun protection and a small backpack)
Note: Parts of the route are narrow with lots of bends

You can walk along the roof of the Olso Opera House

EARLY MORNING ON A ROCKY PLATEAU

Start off in ❶ Stavanger ➤ p. 62. *First drive south to Sandnes and follow Road 13 to the Lauvvik–Oanes ferry.* From the other side, *turn right shortly before Jørpeland to get to Preikestolshytta,* the starting point of the two-hour, strenuous hike to the rocky plateau at ❷ Preikestolen ➤ p. 63. The morning view of Lysefjord is worth getting up early for. Some may also brave the Kjeragbolten, the giant boulder in a crevice 1,000m above the fjord.

VALLEYS, FORESTS AND THE FIRST FERRY

Continue driving on Road 13. Ryfylke is an area full of valleys and forests, narrow fjords with lots of branches and the mountains that extend to the Setesdal in southern Norway. Break the journey at ❸ Årdal. The view over the valley and the village from the old church *(daily 9am–7pm),* an early 17th-century gem, is fantastic. *After crossing the Jøsenfjord by ferry,* enjoy the lovely view stretching eastwards down the fjord from Hjelmeland. Then, *after a short climb, the route continues to the narrow Erfjord and then to Sandsfjord.*

DAY 1		
❶ Stavanger		
	65km	2¼hrs
❷ Preikestolen		
	50km	2hrs
❸ Årdal		
	153km	3½hrs

WATER LEADS THE WAY…

Stay on Road 13 as it heads into the mountains. The stretch along the Suldalsvatnet lake takes you away from the fjords for a while. At Breifonn, you will come to the *E134* that leads to Hardanger ➤ p. 64. The southern landmark of this traditional holiday region is the roaring ❹ Låtefossen waterfall, which crashes into a river next to the road. *Go further north,* and before long you will come to the ❺ Odda Hytte & Gjestegård *(7 rooms, 1 cabin | Jordalsvegen 11B | Odda | tel. 99 27 23 63 | oddahytte. com | £)* where you can spend a relaxing night.

… AND PROVIDES ENERGY

In ❻ Tyssedal, tour the Kraftmuseet or Norwegian Museum of Hydropower and Industry *(early June–early Sept daily 10am–5pm, otherwise shorter opening times | admission 90 NOK | kraftmuseet.no).* The power plant is an impressive construction built between 1900 and 1920 when hydroelectric power became the pillar supporting Norway's energy supply and industrial development.

GIANT BRIDGE OVER THE FJORD

After crossing the gigantic, 1,300m-long hanging bridge over ❼ Hardangerfjord ➤ p. 64, it's not far to ❽ Voss. This winter sports town is a paradise for extreme sport enthusiasts. The meadows on the banks of the Vangsvannet lake in the middle of town are a great place to stop and enjoy the view.

WONDROUS WALK AND A STAVE CHURCH

Soon after you pass by the rushing waters of ❾ Tvindefossen, *the route begins to climb to the pass* of ❿ Vikafjellet. Once you reach the top, stop at the rest area on the southern side of the pass and head off into the mountains for a few hours. *Return to the car and turn left shortly before Vik to the* ⑪ **stave church of Hopperstad (Hopperstad Stavkirke)** *(daily 10am–5pm | admission 80 NOK),* constructed around 1150, whose Gothic altar baldachin is decorated with impressive carvings. *On the other side of the street,* you'll see the small ⑫ **Hove stave church.** Built in the second half of the 12th century, it is the oldest building in the region. This is the last stop before ⑬ **Sognefjord** ➤ *p. 71, which you will now follow for a few minutes to Vangsnes,* where the ferries depart for Hella.

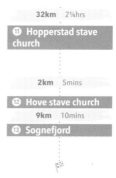

32km	2¼hrs
⑪ **Hopperstad stave church**	
2km	5mins
⑫ **Hove stave church**	
9km	10mins
⑬ **Sognefjord**	

② NORWAY'S DREAM COAST

➤ Look through the hole at Torghatten
➤ Breathe in the scent at Hildur's herb garden
➤ Pay a visit to the Seven Sisters

📍 Steinkjer 🏁 Bodø

→ 940km 🚗 5 days (total driving time 20 hrs)

ⓘ Cost: £235 (fuel, ferry crossings)
Info about Road 17: *kystriksveien.no*

A MOUNTAIN WITH A VIEWING HOLE

Drive north from ❶ **Steinkjer** *to the Holm–Vennesund ferry.* You can see the Torghatten mountain in the distance from the pier in ❷ **Vennesund.** It has a unique feature, namely a hole that the sea has eroded out of the rock. Stay in Vennesund and enjoy the sunset on Nordland's coast. You can find a place to stay at **Vennesund Brygge og Camping** *(3 rorbuers, 15 cabins | tel. 75 02 73 75 | vennesund.no | £).*

The destinations for the next day are ❸ **Brønnøysund** *and* Torghatten, *which you've already admired from*

DAY 1	
❶ **Steinkjer**	
204km	3½hrs
❷ **Vennesund**	
47km	45mins
DAY 2	
❸ **Brønnøysund**	
39km	1hr

afar. The mountain lies on an island 15km to the west. A 20-minute walk will bring you to the hole that is 160m wide and 35m high – plus a marvellous view and fresh sea air await you.

HERBS IN THE HIGH NORTH

8km north of Brønnøysund, a farm is home to the herb garden ❹ **Hildurs Urterarium** *(June–Aug daily 10am–5pm | hildurs.no).* In spite of being so close to the Arctic Circle, they serve tasty herb soup made with ingredients from the garden in the on-site restaurant. *After a 20-minute crossing on the Horn–Anndalsvågen ferry and a lovely 17km stretch along the coast,* you'll come to ❺ **Vevelstad** and ❻ **Forvik**. At the ferry terminal, you'll find the 200-year-old trading post **Forvikgården** and, a little further on, the **local museum** and **church** (1796) with an altarpiece by Joseph Pisani.

POETIC PARSONAGE

Next there's an hour-long ferry ride to Tjøtta. Then drive a further 19km north to ❼ **Alstahaug**, the heart of Nordland. Looking inland, you will see the Seven Sisters mountains. Almost on the lakeshore and next to the 12th-century church, is the residence of the priest and poet Petter Dass (1647–1707) and the impressive **Petter Dass Museum** *(mid-June–mid-Aug daily 10am–5pm, otherwise shorter openings times | admission 120 NOK | petterdass.no).* The main landmark of the fishing town of ❽ **Sandnessjøen** (pop. 5,300) is a 1,000m-long hanging bridge. Plan to spend two nights at the **Rica Hotel Syv Søstre** *(69 rooms | Torolv Kveldulvsonsgate 16 | tel. 75 06 50 00 | rica.no | ££)* to explore the islands of Nordland.

❹ **Hildurs Urterarium**	
28km	45mins
❺ **Vevelstad**	
2km	5mins
❻ **Forvik**	
35km	1½hrs
❼ **Alstahaug**	
21km	25mins
❽ **Sandnessjøen**	

TWO ISLANDS IN THE SEA

Travel with the regular passenger ship on a day trip to the enchanting islands of ❾ Lovund ➤ p. 95 *and* ❿ Træna ➤ p. 95 to visit the hospitable inhabitants who still make their living from fishing and to see the rocks with huge colonies of seabirds.

GLACIAL ADVENTURE

North of Sandnessjøen is the Levang–Nesna ferry. The mountains are now closer to hand. The one-hour *Kilboghamn–Jektvik ferry* is quite special as it crosses the imaginary Arctic Circle. *Just 28km beyond Jektvik you'll reach the Ågskaret–Forøy ferry. The* Engabreen, *a glacier snout of the* Svartisen ➤ p. 95, *has shifted almost to the open sea within the* ⓫ Holandsfjord. You can get close to the crumpled mass of ice on one of the boat tours leaving from Holand or Braset. You can spend the night at the mouth of the fjord with a view of the Norwegian Sea at Furøy Camping *(20 cabins | Halsa | tel. 94 19 13 15 | furoycamp.no | £).*

The old rectory in Alstahaug is decorated with love

IDYLLIC PORT AND STRONG TIDAL CURRENTS

After crossing through the Svartisen tunnel, you'll come to the industrial town of Glomfjord and then Ørnes. A further 38km to the north, take a detour on Road 838 to ⓬ Gildeskål *and walk through the little town to the* church *(guided tours in summer) built before 1250. Enjoy the peace, the idyllic harbour and the fantastic views in all directions. Return to Road 17 and make your way to the turbulent waters of the* ⓭ Saltstraumen ➤ p. 96. Road 17 ends just a few kilometres beyond this maelstrom, which is best viewed from above. *In Løding, turn onto Road 80 to* ⓮ Bodø ➤ p. 92, the end of this route.

DAY 3		
	52km	1hr
❾ Lovund		
	25km	1½hrs
❿ Træna		
	268km	6½hrs
DAY 4		
⓫ Holandsfjord		
	124km	4hrs
DAY 5		
⓬ Gildeskål		
	67km	2½hrs
⓭ Saltstraumen		
	31km	30mins
⓮ Bodø		

❸ FROM OSLO TO A WORLD HERITAGE FJORD

➤ Cycle on the Rallarvegen
➤ Tower over Norway
➤ Enjoy a cool beer at the train station

📍	Oslo	🏁	Bergen
→	530km, 82km of which is a bike tour	🚆	2 days (total train journey 8 hrs)

Cost: £150 (train tickets, bike rental)
What to pack: Bicycle equipment (helmet!)
The cycling route is only viable from mid-July to early September because of snow. Also has some steep inclines
Info about journey/booking info: *fjordtours.com* and *vy.no*

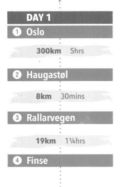

DAY 1

❶ Oslo

300km   5hrs

❷ Haugastøl

8km   30mins

❸ Rallarvegen

19km   1¼hrs

❹ Finse

DAY 2

8km   30mins

❺ Hardangerjøkulen

46km   3hrs

INTO THE MOUNTAINS AND ONTO YOUR BIKE

The train departs ❶ Oslo ➤ p. 42 *in the morning from the main station, carrying you past the cities of Drammen and Hønefoss to the forested valley of Hallingdal. It's all uphill from there* – to the railway station at ❷ Haugastøl, which is about 300km from Oslofjord and 988m higher. Pick up your rental bikes and *tackle the first stretch of the* ❸ Rallarvegen ➤ p. 32. The first part of the route on the old construction road beside the Bergen railway track has a good, although unpaved, path from Haugastøl to ❹ Finse: the "roof of Norway", at an altitude of 1,222m. Spend a night at the Finse Hotel *(43 rooms | tel. 56 52 71 00 | finse1222.no | £££)* and go for an evening stroll along the lakeshore before enjoying the terrace with its glacier view.

The *second stretch of the cycling tour heads downhill, but it is no less challenging.* Even in summer, you can come upon snowdrifts and the weather up here is quite unpredictable. The ❺ Hardangerjøkulen glacier watches over travellers who need to take care on some of the curves, especially after the *Hotel Vatnahalsen*, which marks the start of the *steep decline into the valley*

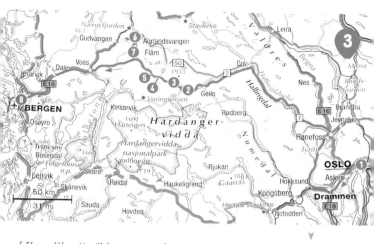

of *Flamsdålen*. You'll have to stay focused on the last 10km because the route descends about 800m and the wind hurtles between the mighty rock walls.

TRAIN TRIP WITH 1,000 TUNNELS AND BENDS

When you arrive at the UNESCO-protected Aurlandsfjord in ❻ Flåm, return your bike at the last station of the world-famous Flåm Railway and have lunch at the popular Ægir microbrewery *(short.travel/nor5 | £)*, which is run by a New Yorker and a Norwegian. If you have time, stop by the Flåmsbahn Museum *(daily | free admission)* in a former station building. Then it's time to *pass through 20 tunnels and around several tight bends back into the mountains on the* ❼ Flåm Railway ➤ p.72. Over a stretch of 20km, the electric train climbs a height of 865m. *In Myrdal, switch over to the Bergen railway and head to the city of Bergen.* You'll pass through the town of Voss and countless tunnels as well as other fjords on the way to ❽ Bergen ➤ p.66. Relax and give yourself time to contemplate an eventful day at the Grand Hotel Terminus *(131 rooms | Zander Kaaesgate 6 | tel. 55 21 25 00 | grandterminus. no | ££)*, a fine hotel with good food near the train station. Bergen is the last stop on this trip through southern Norway.

SIDER TIP
Relax with a craft beer

❻ Flåm

8km   35mins

❼ Flåm Railway

142km   3hrs

❽ Bergen

GOOD TO KNOW

HOLIDAY BASICS

ARRIVAL

AIR

Several airlines offer regular flights from the UK to Norway, some of which are surprisingly cheap. *British Ariways (britishairways.com)* and *SAS (flysas. com)*, as well as the no-frills airlines

Norwegian Air Shuttle (norwegian. com) and *Ryanair (ryanair.com)*, among others, fly out of various British airports to Oslo, Bergen, Haugesund, Stavanger and Trondheim. It's worth noting that "Oslo TORP" is around 120km from central Oslo; the main Gardemoen International airport is much closer and benefits from a fast train service.

There are also a number of flights to Norway from Scotland, in particular from Aberdeen, which service the oil industry.

Flights to and from the US and Canada go via Copenhagen, Stockholm or other European airports.

FERRY

The last car ferry route between the UK and Norway (Newcastle to Bergen) was withdrawn in 2008. However, several ferries operate between Norway and mainland Europe (for example, to

The Hurtigruten ships travel from Bergen to Kirkenes and back again

Denmark). Most operators offer package deals for a car and passengers, and most lines offer concessions. There's usually an additional charge for bicycles and boats.

TRAIN

Travelling from London to Norway by train is possible but takes a long time. If you take a lunchtime *Eurostar* to Brussels, a connecting high-speed train to Cologne, the overnight train to Copenhagen and connecting trains to Oslo, you arrive in the evening the day after leaving London.

An *InterRail Pass* can be recommended for a trip to Scandinavia, available for one month, costing £580 for adults and £446 for young people; or for 22 days, costing £448 for adults and £344 for young people. The eight-day pass costs £248 for adults and £210 for young people. With the pass you can use some bus and ferry lines free of charge and there are reductions on many ferry and bus routes.

GETTING IN

Your luggage will be checked through to your final destination but you must collect it at the first Norwegian airport, take it through customs and hand it in again at a domestic flight counter.

CLIMATE & WHEN TO GO

The climate is the same as the Norwegian countryside: it changes all the time and is rather unpredictable. In a country that stretches for 1,800km and has a mighty mountain range as a weather divide, it comes as no surprise that the east, west, north and south very rarely have the same weather: it's not unusual, for example, to have an Atlantic low in the south but a Siberian high in the north.

Be prepared for rain and soggy ground when you're hiking in the middle of summer. And, even if the weather is calm, make sure that life-jackets, maps and GPS are always at hand when you are on a boat tour.

GETTING AROUND

AIR

For domestic flights, *SAS* flies to the major Norwegian airports and the Dash 8s of the *Widerøe* airline land in the most remote corners of the country. If you plan to travel in summer, it's a good idea to check the internet. *flysas.no | norwegian.no | wideroe.no*.

BUS

Norway has many cross-country, regional and local buses that reach every corner of the country *(nor-way. no).*

CAR

The maximum speed in built-up areas is 50kmh (in residential areas, often 30kmh), on motorways 90kmh, on main roads 80kmh, with a caravan 70kmh (without brakes 60kmh). Dipped headlights are obligatory at all times. The blood alcohol limit is 0.2. It's compulsory for everybody to wear seat belts and children under the age of four require special seats. Passing points on single-lane roads are indicated with an "M". In winter, good winter tyres and snow chains are essential.

For information on closed roads: *tel. 175* (recorded message in Norwegian at the beginning, but don't hang up!) or go to *vegvesen.no/trafikk*

For breakdown assistance: *NAF Automobile Club, tel. 0 85 05*

Toll stations in Norway are usually unstaffed. The *bompenger* ranges from 10 to 160 NOK (for bridges and tunnels). Information about how to pay the toll is provided at most stations in three languages. If you're bringing your own car to Norway, you'll receive an invoice from *EPASS24* before long, but this will be on the highest tariff without discounts. If you get a toll chip, for example from *flyt pass.no* or *fremtindservice.no*, you'll get up to 20 per cent discounted on tolls and 10 per cent on ferry crossings, which is worth it if you're travelling a lot. You can find more information at *autopass.no*

Cities like Oslo or Bergen, in particular, have comparatively high parking charges. The amount depends on the parking zone for petrol/diesel cars (£1.70–£4.30/hr) and electric cars (£0.40–£1.30/hour). Avoid getting a parking fine. If you go over the time you have paid for, you will be fined around £56. Parking within five metres of a junction or a bend is forbidden and there are other parking rules. If you don't observe the rules, you'll be fined £78. Apps like *Easypark* or, in Oslo, *Bil i Oslo* are useful for booking or extending parking easily and for finding free parking spots and charging stations for electric cars.

FESTIVALS & EVENTS
ALL YEAR ROUND

JANUARY
Internationales Filmfestival Tromsø: *tiff.no*

FEBRUARY
Ice Music Festival (Geilo): spherical sound project made of, and in, ice

MARCH/APRIL
Holmenkollen-Skifestival (Oslo): international ski competition, *skifest.no*
Vossajazz (Voss): *vossajazz.no*
★ **Easter Festival** (Kautokeino and Karasjok): Sami festival week filled with many events, including concerts and reindeer races, *samieasterfestival.com*

MAY/JUNE
★ ⚑ **Constitution Day** (17 May, throughout Norway), (photo)
Bergen Festival (Bergen): music from top international artists, *fib.no*
Nattjazz (Bergen): *nattjazz.no*
Middle Ages Festival (Oslo): *oslo middelalderfestival.org*

JUNE
Midsummer Night (Sankthans): with bonfires across the country

JULY
Moldejazz (Molde): internationally famous jazz festival, *moldejazz.no*
Battle of Stiklestad/Olsokdagene (Verdal): "Saint Olav's Play", when he lost his battle for the crown and his life in 1030, *stiklestad.no*

AUGUST
Norland Music Festival (Bodø): classical and jazz, *musikkfestuka.no*
Sildajazz (Haugesund): *sildajazz.no*
Øyafestival (Oslo): open-air rock festival, *oyafestivalen.com*
Notodden Blues Festival (Notodden): *bluesfest.no*

SEPTEMBER
Nuart Festival (Stavanger): street art in the south, *nuartfestival.no*
By:LARM (Oslo): Scandinavian rock & pop newcomers, *bylarm.no*

FERRY

Schedules for the key ferry companies can be found at *norled.no*, *fjord1.no* (mainly for western Norway), *atb.no* (central Norway) and *boreal.no* (northern Norway).

TRAIN

A journey on the Norwegian National Railway network *Vy (vy.no)*, which covers almost 4,300km, can be a lot of fun, especially when travelling long distances. The trains have generous open-plan carriages, and comfortable seats and beds. One-way tickets from Oslo to Bergen are available for 429 NOK if purchased 60 days in advance.

EMERGENCIES

EMBASSIES
BRITISH EMBASSY

Thomas Heftyes Gate 8 | 0244 Oslo | tel. (47) 23 13 27 00 | gov.uk/world/ organisations/british-embassy-oslo

U.S. EMBASSY

Morgedalsvegen 36 | 0378 Oslo | tel. (47) 21 30 85 40 | no.usembassy.gov

CANADIAN EMBASSY

Wergelandsveien 7 (4th floor) | 0244 Oslo | tel. (47) 22 99 53 00 | international.gc.ca/country-pays/norway-norvege

EMERGENCY SERVICES

Police: tel. 112
Fire brigade: tel. 110
Medical emergencies: tel. 113

HEALTH

Almost all medication requires a prescription in Norway. A foreign prescription won't do you any good, so take any important medication you need with you. Headache tablets and nose drops, however, can be bought at the checkout in food shops. All major towns have a community *legevakt* (medical centre).

UK citizens should apply for a free UK Global Health Insurance Card (GHIC) before leaving the UK, which entitles you to state-provided medical treatment. This is not a substitute for private travel insurance, as it does not cover all medical eventualities. Even with a GHIC you'll have to pay the same excess as Norwegians (60 NOK; 280 NOK in the evening or at night). Dentists must be paid in full (350–1,500 NOK). Before they arrive, visitors from all countries should take out comprehensive travel insurance that is suitable for their needs.

There are ticks in Norway *(for info, see fit-for-travel.de)*. However, the fox tapeworm is not common, which means you can pick and eat the blueberries and cloudberries straight off the bush. In the interior and in Finnmark, mosquito nets and a good mosquito cream are essential.

ESSENTIALS

ACCOMMODATION

Hotel rooms are usually cheaper in summer and hotel passes such as the *Fjord Pass* give you additional discounts. But, even if you don't have a pass, it's worth asking for lower rates. In the larger cities, a double room costs 900–1,500 NOK per night, without discount, and an average of 850 NOK in smaller hotels and guesthouses. All hotels provide breakfast buffets.

Gjestgiveri, pensjon and *fjellstue* offer budget stays outside the cities. There are all standards of cabins: the most basic for four to six people costs from 4,000 NOK per week in the off-season (up to 10,000 NOK in the high season). The simplest camping cabin costs 350 NOK per night, larger ones with bath and kitchen cost up to 1,400 NOK.

Rorbus are traditional Norwegian coastal dwellings that stand right on the water. There are a great many on the Lofoten; if you make it that far, you should spend some time in one of the most popular fishing villages in the archipelago: *Henningsvær (tel. 76 06 60 00 | henningsvaer-rorbuer.no)*. If you don't want to drive that far, a beautiful *rorbu* complex can also be found on the island of *Sotra* off the coast of Bergen *(Glesvær Rorbu | tel. 97 11 03 36 | glesver-rorbu.no)*.

There are around 70 hostels in Norway *(vandrerhjem)*. A bed costs from 250 NOK per night for members. Non-members pay an extra 25 NOK. You'll pay from 50 NOK for breakfast or a packed lunch. You can find more information at *hihostels.no (Haraldsheimveien 4 | P.O. Box 53 | Grefsen | 0587 Oslo | info@hihostels.no)*.

HOW MUCH DOES IT COST?

Cappuccino	*about £3.70 per cup*
Sausage	*about £3.00 fried, boiled or grilled, available at almost all petrol stations and at kiosks*
Petrol	*about £1.60 for 1 litre unleaded*
Jumper	*about £85 for a traditional Norwegian jumper*
Beer	*about £8.50 for a 0.5 litre draught beer*
Souvenirs	*about £15 for a small troll figure*

CASH & CREDIT CARDS

Paying with credit card (MasterCard, Visa) in Norway is customary, even for small amounts. If you'd still like to carry cash with you, you can withdraw money from one of the many cash machines (Minibank) with your credit card.

CUSTOMS

It's worth buying things at the duty-free shop: more than half of the 25 per cent VAT will be refunded at the border. Make sure you ask for a Global Refund Cheque when making your purchases. The minimum purchase is 1,000 NOK (excl. VAT) and the goods must be in their original packing.

EU citizens may import and export goods for their own personal use tax-free. Duty-free limits for non-EU citizens are 2 litres of beer, 1.5 litres of wine, 1 litre of spirits and 200 cigarettes. Exporting plants and rare animals (including the eggs of threatened bird species) is forbidden. Exports of fish and fish products are limited to 18kg per person a maximum of twice per calendar year *(toll.no)*.

MEDIA
Many cabins have television and satellite antennas. In the *Narvesen* kiosks in Oslo, Bergen and other major cities, you'll find a selection of English-language newspapers and magazines.

NATIONAL HOLIDAYS

1 Jan.	New Year's Day
28 March 2024, 17 April 2025	Holy Thursday
29 March 2024, 18 April 2025	Good Friday
1 April 2024, 21 April 2025	Easter Monday
1 May	Labour Day
17 May	Constitution Day
9 May 2024, 29 May 2025	Ascension
19 May 2024, 8 June 2025	Whit Monday
25/26 Dec	Christmas (they celebrate on the afternoon of 24 Dec)

OPENING HOURS
Most shops are usually open Monday–Friday from 9am or 10am until 5pm and often close earlier on Saturday. In the cities, most supermarkets are now open Monday–Friday 9am–11pm and Saturday until 6pm. When you're out in the countryside, make sure you stock up on the basics during the regular opening hours, Monday–Friday 9am–5pm, Saturday until 3pm. At other times, the centrally located petrol stations stock a good selection of basic grocery items, plus hot dogs and hamburgers.

INSIDER TIP
Hot dog or petrol?

PHONE
All telephone numbers have eight digits and there are no dialling codes. The code for calling Norway from abroad is 0047. To call other countries from Norway, dial the country code (UK 0044, Ireland 00353, US 001), the dialling code without "0" and then the telephone number. With your mobile phone, dial + instead of the 00 before the country code.

In Norway, there are more mobile phone subscriptions than Norwegians, but renting a phone is complicated and cannot be recommended for tourists.

Check your mobile phone contract before travelling, but there is a cap on mobile roaming charges between Norway and the UK, which allows Norwegians and UK citizens to "Roam like Home" after Brexit.

The most important telephone companies in Norway are *Telenor (telenor.no), OneCall (onecall.no)* and *Telia (telia.no) (all in Norwegian only)*.

PRICES & CURRENCY
One hundred Norwegian kroner (NOK) is the equivalent of around £7.50 or US$9.60. Purchasing power is not one of Norway's strong points and this is particularly apparent when buying food. Having fun is an expensive business, too: half a litre of beer in a pub costs at least 100 NOK, a good meal

390 NOK with an additional 450 NOK for a bottle of wine. You can find an online currency calculator at *oanda.com*

RIGHT TO ROAM

The *allemannsrette* permits everybody to roam freely in the open countryside (unfenced land) – even on private property – and to spend up to two nights there. People, animals and nature must not be disturbed in any way, you must pick up all your rubbish and keep a distance of at least 150m from the nearest inhabited house. Certain sections of the law have been rescinded in some national parks.

TIPS

You should only tip if the service warrants it (maximum: 10 per cent).

Waterfall near Briksdalsbreen glacier station

WEATHER IN OSLO

■ High season
■ Low season

	JAN	FEB	MARCH	APRIL	MAY	JUNE	JULY	AUG	SEPT	OCT	NOV	DEC
Daytime temperature	-2°	-1°	4°	10°	16°	20°	22°	21°	16°	9°	3°	0°
Night-time temperature	-7°	-7°	-4°	1°	6°	10°	13°	12°	8°	3°	-1°	-4°
☀	2	3	4	6	7	8	7	7	5	3	1	1
🌧	8	7	5	7	7	10	11	11	10	10	12	10
≋	3	2	3	5	9	13	16	17	15	11	7	5

☀ Sunshine hours/day   🌧 Rainy days/month   ≋ Water temperature in °C

WORDS & PHRASES IN NORWEGIAN

SMALL TALK

yes/no/maybe	ja/nei/kanskje
Please	Vær så snill
Thank you	Takk
Good morning/day/evening/night	God morgen/dag/kveld/natt
Hello	Hei
Goodbye	Ha det
My name is	Jeg heter ...
What's your name?	Hva heter du?
excuse me	unnskyld meg
sorry	beklager

SYMBOLS

EATING & DRINKING

We'd like to book a table for four for tonight.	**Vi vil gjerne bestille et bord for fire personer til i kveld.**
May I see the menu?	**Kan jeg få menyen?**
May I have … ?	**Kunne jeg få …?**
salt/pepper/sugar	**salt/pepper/sukker**
vinegar/oil	**eddik/olje**
milk/cream/lemon	**melk/fløte/sitron**
with ice/without ice/	**med/uten is**
vegetarian/allergy	**vegetarianer/allergi**
I would like to pay, please.	**Jeg vil gjerne betale.**
cash/credit card	**kontant/kredittkort**
bakery/supermarket	**bakeri/supermarked**

MISCELLANEOUS

Where is …/Where are …?	**Hvor er …?**
What time is it?	**Hva er klokken?**
today/tomorrow/yesterday	**i dag/i morgen/i går**
How much is …?	**Hva koster … ?**
Where is the nearest internet access?	**Hvor er nærmeste internettilgang/ internettilkobling?**
open/closed	**åpent/stengt**
right/left	**høyre/venstre**
pharmacy/perfumery	**apotek/parfymeri**
timetable/ticket	**rutetabell/billett**
broken/out of order	**ødelagt/fungerer ikke**
garage (for car repairs)	**verksted**
ban/banned	**Forbud/forbudt**
Help! Watch out!	**Hjelp!/Pass på!**
0/1/2/3/4/5/6/7/8/9/10/100/1000	**null/en/to/tre/fire/fem/seks/syv/ åtte/ni/ti/hundre/ettusen**

HOLIDAY VIBES
FOR RELAXATION & CHILLING

FOR BOOKWORMS & FILM BUFFS

📖 MY STRUGGLE

Karl Ove Knausgård's six-novel series was completed in 2017 and is an amazing piece of contemporary literature. The question isn't whether you should read it, but when.

🎥 HERE IS HAROLD

Harold (Bjørn Sundquist) feels cheated in life and plans to take revenge by kidnapping the billionaire business magnate and founder of IKEA, Ingvar Kamprad. His amateurish attempts are portrayed in this dark comedy (2016, director: Gunnar Vikene).

📖 THE SNOWMAN

This novel by star Norwegian crime writer Jo Nesbø is packed with suspense and will have you looking over your shoulder. After reading it, you'll see Oslo in a completely different light.

🎥 TROLLHUNTER

Anybody who believes that there are no trolls in Norway is proven wrong in this film (2011), directed by André Øvredal. This parody on the gnarled giants can make you shudder a little – and laugh a lot.

PLAYLIST ON SHUFFLE

⟳ ◄ ❚❚ ►❙ ◄)) ━━━━━━━━━━
                              0:58

❚❚ **BJØRN EIDSVÅG** – MYSTERIET DEG
Popular fixture in the Nordic music scene for decades, singer and songwriter Bjørn Eidsvåg sounds a bit like Donovan – but in Norwegian.

▶ **KINGS OF CONVENIENCE** – MISREAD
Sadly, this Bergen band has now split up, but thankfully their unforgetable sound lives on.

▶ **DUMDUM BOYS** – SPLITTER PINE
Catchy Norwegian rock played in every pub.

▶ **MÁDDJI** – DAWN LIGHT
Sami lyrics and melodies with a modern sound right from the Sami heartland of Kautokeino.

▶ **ALEXANDER RYBAK** – FAIRYTALE
He won the hearts of Europe in the 2009 Eurovision Song Contest with traditional dancing and the Hardanger fiddle.

Your holiday soundtrack can be found on **Spotify** *under* **MARCO POLO Norway**

Or scan this code with the Spotify app

ONLINE

YR
The weather forecasts provided by *yr.no* are the most accurate. Download the app and take it with you.

TAXINÅ!
Regardless of where you are in Norway, you can call a taxi using this app.

A FROG IN THE FJORD
Lorelou Desjardins, a French woman living in Norway, writes about life in the Far North in her English-language blog.

NRKTV – HURTIGRUTE MINUTT FOR MINUTT
Watching a minute-by-minute five-and-a-half-day Hurtigruten trip along the coast makes some fall asleep and is deeply relaxing for others. Claims to be the world's longest TV programme.

YLVIS – THE CABIN
The Ylvis brothers poke fun at the Norwegians' passion for cabins in this self-mocking music video (on YouTube).

TRAVEL PURSUIT
THE MARCO POLO HOLIDAY QUIZ

Do you know what makes Norway tick? Test your knowledge of the idiosyncrasies and eccentricities of the country and its people. The answers are at the foot of the page, with further information on pages 18–23.

❶ Which motifs can be found adorning stave churches?
a) Moose and reindeer
b) Dragons and snakes
c) Goblins and trolls

❷ What's the second most lucrative economic sector for the Norwegians after oil and gas?
a) Norwegian jumpers
b) Timber
c) Aquaculture

❸ What's King Harald's favourite sport?
a) Sailing
b) Archery
c) Mini golf

❹ What are the national colours of the Sami people?
a) Red, blue, yellow, green
b) Yellow, pink, green, white
c) Blue, black, yellow, orange

❺ What's the scientific name for the Northern Lights?
a) Aureola borealis
b) Aurora borealis
c) Aurora borealia

❻ Which of these isn't a Norwegian band name?
a) Röyksopp
b) Kygo
c) Nylo

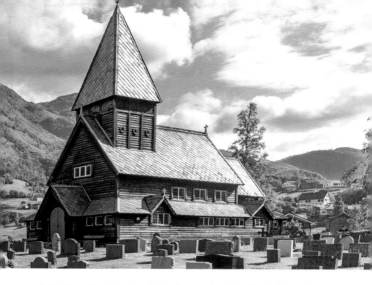

Røldal Stave Church is splendid, but how are the old timber buildings decorated?

❼ What is "korleis"?
a) A fork in the *fjell*
b) The Nynorsk word for "how"
c) A small, tasty fish

❽ What's Jo Nesbø's inspector called?
a) Harry Hole
b) Ole Nordmann
c) Jesper Bringe

❾ What were the Hurtigruten ships originally used for?
a) Ice breakers
b) Expedition ships
c) Postal ferries

❿ Which cities do the Hurtigruten ships travel between?
a) Oslo and Bergen
b) Stavanger and Ålesund
c) Bergen and Kirkenes

⓫ Where can you find Fridtjof Nansen's research ship *Fram*?
a) On Bygdøy museum island in Oslo
b) In endless ice
c) In the garden of a US company with Norwegian roots

⓬ Where do Norwegians get almost 99 per cent of their electricity from?
a) From wind power
b) From nuclear power
c) From hydropower

INDEX

WE WANT TO HEAR FROM YOU!

Did you have a great holiday? Is there something on your mind? Whatever it is, let us know! Whether you want to praise the guide, alert us to errors or give us a personal tip – MARCO POLO would be pleased to hear from you. Please contact us by email:

sales@heartwoodpublishing.co.uk

We do everything we can to provide the very latest information for your trip. Nevertheless, despite all of our authors' thorough research, errors can creep in. MARCO POLO does not accept any liability for this.

PICTURE CREDITS
Cover photo: Stavanger, Preikestolen, Lysefjord (Schapowalow: L. Vaccarella)
Photos: Autorin J. Fellinger (151); DuMont Bildarchiv: U. Bernhart (45, 128/129), Modrow (85); huber-images: U. Bernhart(51), M. Borchi (9), S. Damm (6/7), S. Forster (109), Gräfenhain (100/101, 146/147), F. Lukasseck (110/111), L. Vaccarella (105); Laif: T. Babovic (67, 115), H. Bode (74), C. Boisvieux (127), M. Galli (14/15, 118/119, 124), G. Haenel (19, 70,97), I. C. Hendel (139), B. Jonkmanns (52), M. Kirchgessner (28), S. Multhaupt (30), F. Weiss (27); Laif/Aurora (20); Laif/hemis.fr: E. Berthier (136/137), P. Hauser (31); Look/age fotostock (63); mauritius images: U. Bernhart (8, 83), B. Römmelt (12/13), S. Schurr (148/149), J./D. Warburton-Lee/Pearson (78/79), A. Werth (64); mauritius images/age fotostock (106); mauritius images/Alamy (35, 55, 133), A. Armyagov (88/89), A. K. Beastall (24/25), I. Dagnall (22, 46), C. Fredriksson (87), T. Graham (Klappe hinten), T. Guardia Bencomo (92), Realimage (48), R. Richardson (57), A. Sommer (Klappe vorne aussen, Klappe vorne innen, 1), StockShot (98); mauritius images/ClickAlps: F. Vaninetti (116); mauritius images/imagebroker: M. Dietrich (77), Handl (26), T. Krämer (32/33), A. Schnurer (73); mauritius images/Masterfile RM: J. Schlenker (123); mauritius images/VIEW Pictures (2/3); mauritius images/Westend61: S. Deutsch (11), S. Schurr (38/39); mauritius images/y/Alamy: Parkerphotograph (94/95); shutterstock: giedre vaitekune (10), Smit (58/59)

4th Edition – fully revised and updated 2024
Worldwide Distribution: Heartwood Publishing Ltd, Bath, United Kingdom
www.heartwoodpublishing.co.uk

Authors: Julia Fellinger, Jens-Uwe Kumpch
Editor: Corinna Walkenhorst
Picture editor: Susanne Mack
Cartography: © MAIRDUMONT, Ostfildern (36–37, 130, 132, 135, pull-out map);
© MAIRDUMONT, Ostfildern, using data from OpenStreetMap, licence CC-BY-SA 2.0 (240-41, 43, 60-61, 68, 80-81, 86, 90-91, 102-103, 112-113, 114, 120-121)
Cover design and pull-out map cover design: bilekjaeger_Kreativagentur with Zukunftswerkstatt, Stuttgart
Page design: Langenstein Communication GmbH, Ludwigsburg

Heartwood Publishing credits:
Translated from the German by Sophie Blacksell Jones, Jennifer Walcoff Neuheiser and Samantha Riffle
Editors: Rosamund Sales, Kate Michell, Felicity Laughton
Prepress: Summerlane Books, Bath
Printed in India

MARCO POLO AUTHOR
JULIA FELLINGER
Julia Fellinger is an inherently impatient person, which meant that fishing on the Sognefjord was perfect for her: you just cast your line and then reel it straight back in again. The first time she caught a pollack in 1999, she didn't recognise it and had to look it up in a book. Now the journalist and author of many books on Norway is well versed in fish and has adopted the Norwegians' relaxed approach to life.

DOS & DON'TS

HOW TO AVOID SLIP-UPS & BLUNDERS

DON'T LOAD YOUR CAR UP WITH ALCOHOL
You know that alcohol is going to be expensive in Norway, but don't fill your car with beer! Take a look on *toll.no* to check how much you can import.

DON'T UNDERESTIMATE NATURE
Have you gone the wrong way up the mountain? Wandered away from your boat tour group? Norway's nature isn't an amusement park. It's exciting, sure, but it's also dangerous. Stay informed, plan your trips well and, most importantly, listen to the locals.

DO BE PATIENT
Jostling or pushing in is frowned upon in Norway, queue-jumping even more so. The motto here is *Ta det med ro* (steady does it). Busy places use a *kølapp* system (number system) to regulate the queue. When you're finally called, you can take all the time in the world.

DON'T FISH WITHOUT A SENSE OF PROPORTION
Do you like to fish? Great! But only catch as many as the export restrictions allow (see the "Good to know" chapter). The controls at the border are particularly strict in the summer and the fines are considerable.